Who Am I?
Seeing Myself Through God's Eyes

Valerie Critchlow

Fragrant Storm Collective

Rabbit Trail 1 — Created in God's Image

Genesis 1:27

"So God created man in his own image, in the image of God he created him; male and female he created them."

If I'm going to ask the question Who am I?, I can't ask it honestly without also asking

Whose am I—and why?

Otherwise, the question has no anchor.

It floats aimlessly, which is an invitation for confusion.

Floating questions are easily answered by whatever voice is loudest at the moment.

Scripture doesn't begin by telling me what to do. Scripture begins by telling me who I am—and whose I am. Before I had any role, any responsibility, or any reputation, God created me in His image. That means my life didn't start by being self-defined, and deciding who I was going to be as I traveled the path of my life.

It started with God's intention and clear purpose.

God did not create me randomly. He did not form me accidentally. He created me to reflect something of Himself into the world. He created me to carry His likeness in a way that is uniquely mine, yet unmistakably His.

That thought both humbles me and steadies me, and I appreciate both.

Because if I was created in His image, then my identity is not something I manufacture—it's something I receive. And if I receive it, then my calling is not to invent myself, which would create confusion, but to live in alignment with how He designed me to live, which is settling and reassuring.

I think we often misunderstand what it means to image God well. It doesn't mean pretending. It doesn't mean polishing away our humanity. It doesn't mean performing spiritually for others. It means living authentically, but not selfishly, determining for myself what is "good" and "not good". It means living honestly without compromise, but not harshly toward others. fully myself, but fully surrendered.

When I live according to how God designed me—loving what He loves, walking in truth, extending compassion, choosing humility—I reflect His image more clearly to the confused world around me. When I resist that design, I don't just harm myself; I distort the picture I'm meant to carry into the world.

And yet even here, God's grace meets me.

Because the fullest expression of God's image is never found in my effort—it is found in Christ. Christ is the perfect image of the invisible God. My identity is not merely that I was created in God's image, but that I am invited into Christ, and Christ lives in me.

That is the main trail I always return to.

I am in Christ.

Christ is in me.

And because of Him, God can take every moment of my life—joyful or painful, clear or confusing—and weave purpose into it. Not because I get it right every time, but because His love is relentless, and His design is intentional.

So this rabbit trail brings me back here:

I was created in God's image to glorify Him.
And one of the ways I glorify Him is by imaging Him well—
authentically, humbly, and truthfully—through the life He has
entrusted to me.
Not fake.
Not fractured.
But fully alive in Christ.

Reflective Question

As I sit with God and allow Him to look at me with love, where
might I be carrying ideas about myself that did not come from
Him—and what might change if I let Him gently remind me
whose I am and why He created me?

Prayer

Father,

I come to You quietly, setting down every label, expectation, and
voice that has tried to define me apart from You. I want to see
myself the way You see me—not through fear or comparison,
but through Your truth and Your love. Remind me that I am Yours,
that I was created in Your image with intention and care. Where I
have forgotten who I am, bring clarity. Where I have tried to
define myself apart from You, bring rest. Shape my heart so that
my life reflects You—not by pretending, but by living honestly
and surrendered. Thank You that my identity is secure in Christ,
and that You are patient as I learn to live from that truth.
Amen

Rabbit Trail 2 — Known Before I Knew
Jeremiah 1:5 (NLT)
"I knew you before I formed you in your mother's womb.
Before you were born I set you apart
and appointed you as my prophet to the nations."

I've been sitting with this verse, and I keep coming back to one
simple thought:
God didn't just know about me.
He knew me.
Not in a distant, factual way. Not like collecting information. He
knew my very being. He knew my nature. My purpose. My wiring.
I may have been a surprise to my parents—but I was no
surprise to God.
Before He ever formed me in the womb, I was already known by
my Creator. Known at a depth no human could reach, even if they
spent an entire lifetime trying. He knows me more fully than I
could ever know myself.
And I think I understand that more clearly because I'm a potter.
When I sit down to make a vessel, I don't just grab a random lump
of clay and hope something good comes out of it. Before I ever
touch the wheel, I already know what I'm making. I know the kind
of vessel I have in mind. I know roughly how much clay it will
take. I cut that amount free first—before I wedge it, before I
center it, before it ever starts to take shape.

The weight matters.
The clay body matters.
The purpose matters.
I already know whether this piece is meant to hold water, or food, or simply beauty. That decision shapes everything that comes next. It determines how I form it, how thick the walls need to be, what kind of glaze I can use, and how it will be fired. There are glazes I would never use on a vessel meant for nourishment— and others that are perfectly safe and suited for that purpose. I'm thinking about the end use long before the piece ever exists. And the more I think about it, the more I realize—that's how God planned for me.

It was never a question of whether I would be a vessel. He created me, so I am one by design. But He knew what kind of vessel I was meant to be. He knew the weight, the shape, the purpose. He knew what I would be used for and what I would not. He knew the kind of forming it would take—and the kind of refining I could handle.

That reframes everything for me.

Because my life was never meant to be a wandering experiment. I wasn't created to drift through my days trying to figure out how to spend my time or wondering whether I matter. My every moment carries purpose—not because I always recognize it, but because God already does.

This promise wasn't only for Jeremiah. His calling was unique, but the truth behind it is universal for those who have surrendered their lives to Christ. When Christ lives in me and I live in Him, my life is not accidental. I am known. I am set apart. I am formed with intention.

And when I live surrendered to my Creator, even the ordinary moments become meaningful. Even the waiting has shape. Even the unseen seasons are part of the design.

So this rabbit trail brings me back to the main trail again.

My identity is not rooted in my ability to figure myself out.

It is rooted in the God who knew me before He ever formed me.

And that knowing finds its fullest expression in Christ.

Christ in me.

Me in Christ.

God's redemptive purpose at work in every moment of my life —even the ones I don't yet understand.

Reflective Question

As I sit with God, where might I be questioning my purpose or shape—and what might change if I trusted that He knew exactly what kind of vessel He was forming before my life ever began?

Prayer

Father,

Thank You for knowing me so completely—before I had words, before I had form, before I ever questioned my place in the world. Thank You that my life was not an accident and my days are not wasted. Help me trust Your hands when I don't understand the shaping. When I feel unfinished or uncertain, remind me that You are a careful and intentional Creator. I surrender myself to You again, asking You to keep forming me in ways that reflect Your purpose and Your love. Let my life be a vessel that brings nourishment, truth, and grace to the world around me.

Amen

Rabbit Trail 3 — Fearfully and Wonderfully Made
Psalm 139:13–14 (NLT)
You made all the delicate, inner parts of my body
and knit me together in my mother's womb.
Thank you for making me so wonderfully complex!
Your workmanship is marvelous—how well I know it.

When I sit with Psalm 139 and let it breathe for a while, I find myself smiling. "Fearfully and wonderfully made." Wonderfully complex. Marvelous workmanship. Those words don't feel distant or abstract to me. They feel familiar.

I'm a creative. And whenever I'm creating something—anything—I'm all in.

If I'm designing a game for my kids or grandkids, I'm thinking about it constantly. If I'm sewing a dress, sketching a watercolor illustration, building a new program, designing a health protocol tailored for one specific person, or even rearranging a room so it functions better, my mind is wrapped around it. Even while I'm doing laundry or cooking dinner or carrying on a conversation, part of me is still thinking through the design.

How will this work?

What does it need?

What would make it stronger?

What would make it beautiful and useful at the same time?

If I know someone will be on my massage table tomorrow with a specific injury or dysfunction, I don't stop thinking about it. I'll be gardening, cleaning, cooking—and in the background of my mind, I'm tracing muscle attachments and bony landmarks, thinking through how one muscle group interacts with another, how the kinetic chain works together. I'm already imagining how to help restore what isn't functioning as it was designed to function.

And that's just me.

So when I read that God knit me together... that He made me wonderfully complex... that His workmanship is marvelous... I can't help but imagine His full attention.

Not distracted.

Not hurried.

Not improvising.

Focused.

Intent on creating me in a very specific way. Knowing exactly what He was doing. Not stopping until I was precisely the way He wanted me to be—the exact way He wanted Himself to be imaged through me.

That thought brings me comfort. It gives me those warm, steady feelings of being treasured. Because if I, in my limited humanity, can pour that much attention into something I create, how much more would the Creator of everything pour His perfect wisdom, love, and intention into forming me?

He didn't just make a generic human and hope I'd turn out fine.

He formed me so that His character, His beauty, His strength, His compassion could be reflected uniquely through my life.

If I can keep that truth at the front of my thoughts—that I was created on purpose, with purpose, to image Him accurately—it steadies my identity.

When I forget it, I become critical. I compare. I let other people's opinions define my value. I set perfectionist standards that don't even match what God designed me for. I try to measure myself against something that was never meant to be my frame.

But when I remember that I am His workmanship, that He intentionally designed me, grace shows up. Grace for my weaknesses. Grace for my growth process. Grace for the fact that I am still being shaped.

If I keep my perception framed by His design instead of by human opinion, I don't struggle nearly as much with imaging Him well. Because I'm no longer striving to be impactful—I'm simply being faithful.

And when I image Him well—when it becomes evident that I am in Christ and Christ is in me—impact takes care of itself. I don't have to orchestrate it. I don't have to force it. I don't have to curate an image.

I simply live surrendered.

And in that surrender, God's redemptive purpose moves through every conversation, every challenge, every ordinary moment.

If I can remember that I am fearfully and wonderfully made— not by accident, not by chance, but by the focused attention of my Creator—then I think I've got it made.

Not because life is easy.
But because my identity is settled.
Christ in me.
Me in Christ.
God's workmanship still unfolding.

Reflective Question
If I truly believed that I was intentionally designed by God to image Him uniquely, how would that change the way I see myself today—especially in the areas where I tend to be most critical?

Prayer
Father,
Thank You for forming me with intention. Thank You that I am not random, not overlooked, not assembled carelessly. Your workmanship is marvelous, even when I struggle to see it. Help me keep Your design at the front of my thoughts. Guard me from measuring myself by standards that are smaller than Your purpose. Teach me to receive Your grace and to extend that same grace to myself. Let Christ in me reflect You clearly. Let my life—just as it is today—be part of Your beautiful, redemptive work. I am grateful to be Your workmanship.
Amen

Rabbit Trail 4 — In His Image, Not Mine

Colossians 1:15 (NLT)

"Christ is the visible image of the invisible God. He existed before anything was created and is supreme over all creation."

There are moments — more than I'd like to admit — when I don't deliberately reject God… I just quietly shrink Him.
Not on purpose. Not rebelliously. Just in the way my mind tries to make sense of everything.
I imagine Him reacting like I would react.
I interpret His silence like human silence.
I measure His patience by the limits of my own.
And without realizing it, I begin to fit God into the image of a man — instead of remembering that man was created in the image of God.
That reversal is subtle, but it changes everything.
Because the moment I shrink Him to something I can fully explain, I'm no longer being shaped by Him. I'm shaping Him.
And a God I can completely explain isn't really God.
I think about measurements. If someone tells me a piece of fabric needs to be thirty-two centimeters across, but I cut it using inches in my head, I may think I've measured carefully — but I've used the wrong standard. The result won't match the intention. The flaw won't be in the fabric. It will be in my measuring.
Sometimes I do that with God.

I measure Him with human tools — human logic, human emotion, human limitation — and then I wonder why my understanding feels off. Why my peace feels thin. Why my identity feels slightly distorted.

If I reduce God to something manageable, then my view of myself will shrink too. Because I can only image Him as accurately as I see Him.

But Christ.

Christ is the visible image of the invisible God.

If I want to know what God is like, I look at Jesus.

Not my assumptions.

Not my projections.

Not my cultural lens.

Jesus.

Holy and compassionate.

Strong and gentle.

Truthful and merciful.

Unexplainable and yet deeply personal.

He does not fit neatly into my categories. And that's good. I would never want to worship a God small enough to fit inside my understanding. The moment He becomes fully explainable, He becomes human-sized.

And I was not created to image something human-sized.

I was created to image Him.

When I see God clearly — through Christ — I begin to understand myself clearly. Not as the measure, but as the reflection. Not as the source, but as the vessel. Not as the definition of truth, but as one shaped by it.

This rabbit trail brings me right back to the main path.
My identity is not rooted in how well I can explain God.
It is rooted in Christ who reveals Him.
Christ in me.
Me in Christ.
And because of Him, even my misunderstandings can be corrected.
Even my distorted perceptions can be healed. Even my small
measurements can be replaced with His eternal standard.
God is not asking me to fully comprehend Him.
He is inviting me to trust Him — and to let Him define Himself.
When I do that, I begin to image Him more purely.
And that is where identity steadies.

Reflective Question
Where in my life might I be unconsciously measuring God by
human standards — and how might my identity shift if I allowed
Christ to redefine my understanding of who God truly is?

Prayer

Father,

I come to You honestly. There are moments when I shrink You without meaning to. When I interpret You through my fears, my experiences, or my limited understanding. Forgive me for fitting You into categories that feel comfortable but fall short of who You truly are. Reveal Yourself to me through Christ. Correct what I have mismeasured. Expand what I have reduced. Help me see You clearly — not as I imagine You to be, but as You are. And as I see You rightly, shape my identity through that truth. Let Christ in me reflect You faithfully. Let every moment of my life — even this one — be part of Your redemptive work in me and through me.

Amen

Rabbit Trail 5 — You Are Not an Accident

Psalm 127:3 (NLT)

Psalm 127:3 tells us that children are a heritage from the Lord—offspring are a reward from Him.

A reward.

A gift.

I've been thinking about that word.

Not an accident.

Not a burden.

Not a mistake.

A reward.

Now, I was a surprise to my parents. My mom was sixteen years old. My dad lived in another state. On paper, I might have looked inconvenient. Unplanned. Unexpected.

But never—not once—did I hear even a hint of regret from either of them. They treasured me from the moment they knew I existed. They could have responded differently. They didn't. And I am deeply grateful.

That made it easier for me to see myself as a gift.

But I know that isn't everyone's story.

Some people grew up hearing words that suggested they were unplanned... or inconvenient... or a burden. Some have felt like they showed up at the wrong time or in the wrong place. Some have carried the quiet weight of feeling unwanted.

So let me say this clearly.

You may have been a surprise to your parents.

But you were no surprise to God.

You were not an accident.

You were not an oversight.

You were not a miscalculation.

You were a gift.

Regardless of how you were first received, you were intentionally created to image God. You were formed with purpose. You were entrusted to the world as a reward.

And nothing that has happened to you has reduced your value.

I think about a hundred-dollar bill. If I hand someone a crisp, clean hundred-dollar bill, they're thrilled. If I wrinkle it up, stuff it in my pocket, and hand it to them, they still want it. If I drop it in the mud, let trucks run over it all day, and then pick it up—dirty, crumpled, barely recognizable—it is still worth one hundred dollars.

Its value never changed.

Only its condition did.

And God is very good at cleaning up hundred-dollar bills.

Nothing you've walked through—no disappointment, no rejection, no mistake, no regret—has diminished your worth. You may feel wrinkled. You may feel muddy. You may feel like you've been run over by life more than once.

But your value was set by your Creator. And He does not revise His declarations.

You are a heritage.

You are a reward.

You are treasured.

And not only by the One who made you.

When you walk in the quiet confidence that you are of extreme value—not arrogant, not self-inflated, just settled—you begin to image Him well. You stop striving to prove yourself. You stop shrinking to make others comfortable. You stop believing that your past has erased your purpose.

Christ in you.

You in Christ.

That is where your value is secured. Not in how you were received. Not in how well you performed. Not in how others measured you.

God's redemptive work does not reduce value. It restores clarity.

You were never an accident.

You are a gift.

And when you believe that, you begin to live like it.

Reflective Question

If I truly believed that I am a gift—intentionally created and permanently valuable—how would that change the way I see myself today, especially in the places where I have felt diminished?

Prayer

Father,

Some days it's easier to see my flaws than my value. Some days I remember the mud more than the worth. Remind me that my value was set by You, not by circumstances, not by people, not even by my own mistakes. If I have believed that I am less because of what I've been through, gently correct that lie. Reassure me that You are not surprised by my story and that nothing has reduced my worth in Your eyes. Thank You for treasuring me. Thank You for calling me a gift. Help me walk in that truth—with humility, with confidence, and with trust in Your redemptive love.

Amen

Rabbit Trail 6 — Image Bearers, Still
Genesis 3:8–10 (NLT)

"When the cool evening breezes were blowing, the man and his wife heard the Lord God walking about in the garden. So they hid from the Lord God among the trees. Then the Lord God called to the man, 'Where are you?' He replied, 'I heard you walking in the garden, so I hid. I was afraid because I was naked.'"

When God created man and woman, He created them in His image and after His likeness. Everything else in creation came into being at the sound of His voice. But humanity was different. Formed. Breathed into. Intimate.

Scripture also tells us that God is clothed in light. That image lingers with me.

If He is clothed in light, and we were created in His image, it's not hard for me to imagine that Adam and Eve carried a kind of radiant covering as well. Not something stitched or sewn. Not something external and artificial. Something that simply flowed from being in perfect union with Him.

Light doesn't need fabric.

When a light bulb is glowing, you don't see the mechanics inside it. You see the glow. The inner workings are hidden by brilliance. But the moment the light goes out, everything inside is suddenly visible — exposed. The filament, the structure, the parts that were always there but unseen.

And I wonder.
When Adam and Eve chose autonomy — choosing for themselves
what was good and evil instead of trusting God to define it —
did the light dim?
Not because God stripped them.
But because separation dims what connection illuminates.
If their light dimmed, exposure would have followed. Suddenly
aware of their vulnerability. Suddenly self-conscious. Suddenly
hiding.
"I was afraid because I was naked."
Fear entered where trust had been.
Hiding entered where communion had been.
Exposure entered where light had covered.
And yet — here's what steadies me — even after that moment,
they were still image bearers.
Fallen, yes.
Frightened, yes.
Hiding, yes.
But still created in His image.
The image wasn't erased. It was marred.
And that means something for me.
There are times when I feel exposed — aware of flaws, aware of
weakness, aware of parts of me that don't feel radiant at all.
Times when I would rather hide than be seen. Times when I have
tried to define good and evil for myself instead of trusting God.
But the image of God in me has not been erased.

And here is the beauty that brings me back to the main trail:
Christ.
If separation dimmed the light, Christ restores it. If fear caused
hiding, Christ calls me out by name. If autonomy fractured
communion, Christ bridges it.
Christ in me.
Me in Christ.
The light is not self-generated. It never was. It has always been
borrowed brilliance — reflected glory.
And even when I feel exposed, I am still an image bearer. Still
pursued. Still called. Still invited out of hiding.
God didn't walk into the garden in Genesis 3 to condemn. He
walked in to call.
"Where are you?"
Not because He didn't know.
But because relationship still mattered.
Image bearers, still.

Reflective Question
Where in my life have I been hiding — feeling exposed,
diminished, or dimmed — and what might change if I
remembered that I am still an image bearer, still pursued, still
invited back into the light?

Prayer

Father,

There are moments when I feel exposed and small, aware of my weakness and quick to hide. Thank You that Your image in me has not been erased. Thank You that even when I have chosen my own understanding over Yours, You still call my name. Restore what has dimmed. Draw me out of hiding. Help me trust that Your light is not meant to shame me, but to clothe me again in Your presence. Let Christ in me reflect Your glory, not my fear. I choose to step back into Your light.

Amen

Rabbit Trail 7 — The Voice of Shame

Genesis 3:11–12 (NLT)

"Who told you that you were naked?" the Lord God asked. "Have you eaten from the tree whose fruit I commanded you not to eat?"

The man replied, "It was the woman you gave me who gave me the fruit, and I ate it."

There is something in that first question that stops me every time.

"Who told you…?"

Not Why did you…?

Not How could you…?

Not even What is wrong with you?

But — Who told you?

Somewhere between the choice and the hiding, a new voice entered the garden.

Before that moment, Adam and Eve were naked and unashamed. After that moment, they were afraid. They covered. They hid. They blamed.

Nothing about their physical bodies had changed. What changed was what they believed about themselves.

Shame had entered.

And I've come to understand something in my own life:

Shame is not the voice of God.

Conviction? Yes.

Guilt? Sometimes, yes.

A pricking of conscience when I've deliberately chosen my own understanding instead of trusting His? Absolutely.

But shame — the heavy, suffocating voice that says, You are your failure. You are your mistake. You are less now — that is not Him.

Conviction draws me toward restoration.

Shame pushes me into hiding.

Conviction says, Let's fix this. Come closer.

Shame says, Cover up. Stay away.

In the garden, after autonomy replaced trust, fear followed. And fear does strange things. It fractures trust — with God, with each other, even within ourselves. If I've chosen less than God's best, then suddenly I don't trust my own judgment. I don't trust the other person involved. And worst of all, I begin to mistrust God's heart toward me.

That's when hiding feels safer than honesty.

But listen carefully to what God does not do in Genesis 3.

He does not shame them.

He asks a question.

He already knew the answer. He could see the inner workings of the "light bulb" long before the glow dimmed. He wasn't discovering anything new about them. He was inviting them into awareness.

That is conviction.

Conviction is not humiliation. It is clarity with hope attached. Shame, on the other hand, is condemnation without remedy. It wants to define me by my lowest moment. It wants to distort my identity until I forget who I am and whose I am.

And here is the truth that steadies me:

My identity does not change because I chose poorly.

My standing in Christ is not revoked because I temporarily believed a lesser voice.

There is no condemnation in Jesus.

If I begin to see myself as my shortcomings — if I start labeling myself by my sin, my reaction, my doubt — then shame has quietly taken the microphone.

But when I ask God, "Show me myself through Your eyes," something shifts.

He shows me a daughter.

He shows me one who is growing.

He shows me one already covered — not in fig leaves, but in grace.

Conviction becomes a beautiful thing then. It becomes a turning point, not a tombstone. It becomes the place where I crawl up into His lap and say, "I chose less than what You offered. Help me choose differently next time."

And He does not push me away.
He draws me in.
The enemy uses shame to control.
God uses conviction to restore.
Shame says, You are dirty.
Conviction says, You wandered. Let's wash up and walk forward.
And because I am in Christ and Christ is in me, restoration is not
a possibility — it is a promise.
Shame does not get to dominate my story.
Grace does.
Even in the garden, God was already moving toward redemption.
And every time I fall short, He is still moving toward restoration
— not with condemnation, but with mercy.
What gratitude fills me when I realize I don't have to hide.

Reflective Question
When I feel the weight of my mistakes, do I hear the voice of
shame telling me who I am — or do I pause long enough to ask,
"Who told me that?" and allow God to show me myself through
His gracious eyes?

Prayer

Father,

There have been moments when I have hidden. Moments when I have believed that my failure defined me. Thank You for asking gentle questions instead of speaking harsh condemnation. Thank You that Your conviction carries grace, not shame. When the voice of shame tries to label me by my lowest choices, remind me of who I am in Christ. Show me myself through Your eyes. Clean what needs cleaning. Restore what needs restoring. And thank You — truly thank You — that I never have to hide from You. I choose to come closer instead.

Amen

Rabbit Trail 8 — Covered by God
Genesis 3:21
[21] And the Lord God made garments of skin for Adam and his wife, and clothed them.

They had just blown it.
Not just a small misstep. Not a technicality. They had chosen autonomy over trust. They had decided to define good and evil for themselves instead of receiving it from the One who is goodness itself.
And the consequences were enormous. Not just for them — for everyone who would come after them. The fracture would ripple through every generation.
If anyone had the right to rage, it was God.
But what did He do?
He covered them.
He did not leave them in their exposed shame. He did not force them to walk the rest of their days constantly humiliated, naked reminders of their failure. He did not revoke their image-bearing status. He did not scream or shame or withdraw His presence.
He made garments of skin for them.
Something innocent died so that they could be covered.
That is not a small detail.
Up until that moment, there had been no death. And now, because of their choice, death entered the story. Animals who had done nothing wrong were sacrificed so that Adam and Eve would not remain exposed.

Their sin had consequences. God did not pretend it didn't. But He also did not abandon them to it.

He covered them.

It tells me something about the heart of God. Even in betrayal. Even in heartbreak. Even when His image-bearers choose less than what He lovingly provided.

He is not a God who delights in shame.

He is a God who covers.

He is a God who provides a way.

He is a God who says, "Yes, there are consequences. But you are still Mine."

The enemy wields shame skillfully. He whispers, "Look what you've done. Look what you've unleashed. Look who you are now."

But God's voice rises above that.

"You are still Mine. You still bear My image. You are still part of My story."

The covering in Genesis was temporary. Skin garments. Necessary. Costly. But temporary.

And from that moment on, the story unfolds the same way over and over again. Humanity wanders. Humanity wounds. Humanity forgets. And God provides covering.

Sacrifices. Covenants. Mercy. Rescue.

The entire arc bends toward Jesus.

Because the skins in the garden were only the beginning. They were a shadow. A whisper of something greater.

Eventually, the covering would not be animal skins.

It would be Christ.

Christ, who was sinless...became sin...for other humans that would repeatedly continue to sin, and fall into ingratitude. Christ, who took shame without returning shame. Christ, whose sacrifice was not temporary but complete.

God has been covering His people since the beginning.

Not excusing.

Not ignoring.

But covering.

And when I think about my own life — the places I have chosen autonomy, the places I have trusted my understanding over His — I am overwhelmed with gratitude that His response is not abandonment.

It is provision.

It is restoration.

It is grace that costs Him something but restores me everything.

I am covered.

Not because I hid well.

Not because I performed well.

But because He loves well.

And so this rabbit trail circles back to the main path again.

God and His people.

God for His people.

God writing redemption into every generation.

Christ in me.

Me in Christ.

Covered. Not condemned.

Restored. Not erased.

Reflective Question
Where in my life do I still feel exposed or defined by past failure — and what might change if I truly believed that God has already provided covering through Christ?

Prayer
Father,

Thank You for covering me. Thank You that Your first response to failure was not rejection but provision. I am humbled that from the very beginning, You made a way. Where I still carry shame, remind me that I am covered. Where I still try to hide, draw me out gently. Thank You for the cost You were willing to bear so that I would not remain exposed. Thank You for Jesus — the final and perfect covering. I receive Your grace again today with gratitude. I am Yours, covered and loved.

Amen

Rabbit Trail 9 — God's Pursuit Has Always Been Personal

Isaiah 43:1 (NLT)

But now, O Jacob, listen to the Lord who created you.

O Israel, the One who formed you says,

"Do not be afraid, for I have ransomed you.

I have called you by name; you are mine."

I cannot get over that sentence.

I have called you by name; you are Mine.

He said that to a people who were inconsistent.

Fearful.

Distrusting.

Unfaithful.

Wandering.

And He says it to me knowing I am sometimes all of those things too.

What undoes me is this: my inconsistency does not change my identity.

When I fall short, I do not fall out of being His.

When I am fearful, I do not cease being called.

When I am untrusting, He does not retract His claim.

He does not love me less.

He does not pursue me less.

He does not step back and say, "Come see Me when you've figured it out."

He continues to say, Mine.

But here's what I've had to admit in quiet honesty:

While my identity does not change, my experience does.

When I choose fear over trust, my life feels less than what it could be.

When I cling to control instead of surrender, my days feel tighter, smaller, more chaotic.

When I resist His leading, I don't lose Him — but I do experience less than the fullness He intends.

It isn't punishment.

It isn't Him pulling away.

It's simply that fear produces less than peace.

Distrust produces less than rest.

Autonomy produces less than abundance.

There is "more than."

There is "equal to."

And there is "less than."

He is always offering the more than.

When I choose differently, I step into less than.

But even there — even in the less than — He is still calling my name.

Still pursuing.

Still redeeming.

Still wooing.

He doesn't wait until I improve to move toward me.
He moves toward me in the middle of my inconsistency.
He is not standing at a distance with crossed arms.
He is leaning in, saying, "Do not be afraid... you are Mine."
That means my missteps may affect my experience of the
journey, but they do not cancel the journey.
They may bring chaos, but they do not remove His claim.
They may shrink my peace, but they do not shrink His love.
And that realization changes the way I see my failures.
Instead of seeing them as evidence that I don't belong, I can see
them as invitations back into fullness.
Back into trust.
Back into peace.
Back into the "more than" He has always offered.
Because my identity was never built on my consistency.
It was built on His.
And so I come back to the main trail again:
I am in Christ.
Christ is in me.
God's pursuit of me is deeply personal.
Even when I get it wrong.
Especially when I get it wrong.
He calls me by name.
And I am His.

Reflective Question

Where in my life right now am I living in "less than" — not because God has withdrawn, but because I have been walking in fear, control, or mistrust? What would it look like to return to His "more than" without shame, simply because I am already His?

Prayer

Father,

You call me by name even when I am inconsistent.

You do not withdraw when I waver.

You do not love me less when I fall short.

You do not pause Your pursuit until I improve.

Thank You.

Forgive me for believing that my failures change who I am to You.

Forgive me for shrinking back when You are actually leaning in.

Help me see the difference between identity and experience.

When I choose fear and it produces chaos, remind me that I am not being punished — I am being invited back into trust.

When I walk in less than, remind me that more than is still available.

You are not waiting for me to get it right.

You are calling me closer.

You are still saying, "You are Mine."

Let that truth steady my heart.

Let it quiet my fear.

Let it draw me back into the fullness You always intended.

I am Yours.

And You are not letting go.

Amen

Rabbit Trail 10 — Created From Overflow

There is something that changes everything for me when I really sit with this:

God did not create humanity because He needed us.

He was not lonely.

He was not incomplete.

He was not lacking something in eternity.

We were not a necessity.

We were an overflow.

Isaiah 43:7 (NLT)

Bring all who claim me as their God, for I have made them for my glory. It was I who created them.

Created for His glory.

That doesn't make us small.

That makes us radiant.

And then this:

Revelation 4:11 (NLT)

"You are worthy, O Lord our God, to receive glory and honor and power. For you created all things, and they exist because you created what you pleased."

We exist because it pleased Him.

Not because He required help.

Not because He ran out of options.

Because it delighted Him.

And when I layer that with this:
I John 4:8, 19 (NLT)
But anyone who does not love does not know God, for God is love.
We love each other because he loved us first.
God is love.
Love, by its nature, gives.
Love shares.
Love overflows.
So creation itself is generosity. He created not from deficiency, but from abundance. He wanted to share His glory. He wanted to share joy. He wanted to share life itself.
And then I think about something else.
When He rescued His people from slavery in Egypt and gave them the Law, it wasn't to restrict them.
We often hear "law" and think limitation.
But His law was protection.
It was guidance.
It was love put into boundaries.
Had they lived inside that framework willingly and trustingly, they would have been spared so much of the disease, chaos, moral decay, and heartache that surrounded the nations around them.
He didn't withhold what was good.
He withheld what was destructive.
The only things He kept them from were the very things that would enslave them again.
That reframes everything.

When I made rules in my home as our children were growing up,
it wasn't because I enjoyed restriction. I would have loved to live
without them — and they would have too.
But I knew something they didn't yet understand:
They could not walk in fullness of joy, safety, and real freedom
without boundaries.
Those boundaries weren't there to keep them from anything
good.
They were there to allow them to live freely within everything
good.
That is exactly what God was doing.
Even His law was an overflow of love.
Even His "no" was generosity.
Even His "draw back" was protection.
Even His "move forward" was invitation into fullness.
He didn't create us and then set up a maze of restrictions to
test us.
He created us for relationship.
John 17:3 (NLT)
And this is the way to have eternal life—to know you, the only
true God, and Jesus Christ, the one you sent to earth.
Eternal life is knowing Him.
Communion.
Closeness.

Revelation 3:20 shows Him standing at the door and knocking.
Ezekiel 37:27 speaks of Him dwelling with His people.
From Genesis to Revelation, the thread is steady:
He wants to be with us.
In Genesis, when He created humanity in His image and gave them
dominion, He wasn't hiring managers.
He was inviting children into shared life.
If He could speak galaxies into existence, He did not need help
tending a garden.
He invited us into stewardship because partnership is part of love.
Everything He does flows from who He is.
And He is love.
That means even correction is love.
Even structure is love.
Even boundaries are love.
Even purpose is love.
We were created from overflow — not obligation.
And every invitation He gives us, every guardrail He sets, every
direction He provides, is meant to keep us within the wide-open
space of true freedom.
Not slavery.
Freedom.
I exist because it pleased Him.
I was created to reflect Him.
I was invited into communion with Him.
And even when He asks me to draw back from something, it is
not to diminish my life — it is to protect the fullness of it.
That is generosity beyond comprehension.

Reflective Question
Where have I mistaken God's boundaries for restriction instead of
protection — and how might my perspective shift if I truly
believed every "no" from Him was guarding something better?

Prayer
Father,
It amazes me that You didn't create me because You needed me.
You created me because You wanted to share Yourself.
You are love — and love overflows.
Forgive me for ever seeing Your boundaries as limitation instead
of protection. Forgive me for bristling at Your law instead of
recognizing it as kindness.
You have never kept me from anything good.
You have only guarded me from what would enslave me.
Help me trust Your heart.
Help me rest inside the space You've created for me to flourish.
Thank You for wanting relationship. Thank You for inviting me into
shared purpose. Thank You that even Your structure is generosity.
I am here because it pleased You.
And everything You ask of me is rooted in love.
Amen

Rabbit Trail II — Called By Name
Isaiah 45:3 (NLT)
And I will give you treasures hidden in the darkness—
secret riches.
I will do this so you may know that I am the Lord,
the God of Israel, the one who calls you by name.
Treasures hidden in the darkness.
If I'm honest, I don't like that phrase at first glance.
I would prefer treasures hidden in abundance.
Treasures hidden in celebration.
Treasures hidden in seasons where everything feels steady and
bright.
But that isn't what He says.
He says the treasures are hidden in the dark.
And when I look back over my life, I can see it. There are things I
learned in grief that I never could have learned in ease. There are
depths of intimacy with Him that only surfaced when everything
else crumbled. There were seasons when the darkness felt so thick
I was sure it would swallow me whole — and yet, somehow, that
was where I discovered Him in ways I never had before.
There were riches stored there.
Not riches I would have chosen.
Not lessons I would have signed up for.
But treasures nonetheless.

There were truths about His nearness that could only be found when I had nowhere else to turn. There were revelations about His faithfulness that only became visible when the path ahead was invisible. There were parts of my own heart that were refined, steadied, and strengthened in the valley — treasures I might have gone my entire life without uncovering had I avoided the dark.

And here's the part that undoes me:

"I will do this so you may know... the one who calls you by name."

Not "calls humanity."

Not "calls His creation."

Calls you.

Calls me.

By name.

Out of billions.

Out of generations stacked upon generations.

He calls me.

When the darkness threatens to define me, He calls me by name.

When fear rises.

When frustration overwhelms.

When I feel small, unseen, replaceable.

He calls me by name.

He does not diminish who I am. He does not flatten me into "just another human." He knows everything about me — every weakness, every strength, every fear, every gift, every moment of doubt — and still, He calls me specifically into more.

More alignment.
More surrender.
More purpose.
More intimacy.
And He doesn't call me away from who I am — He calls me
deeper into who He created me to be.
He uses my wiring.
He uses my story.
He uses my temperament.
He uses even the seasons that hurt.
He calls me out of the valley of the shadow of death and into love.
He calls me out of judgment and into grace.
He calls me out of fear and into trust.
Not generically.
Personally.
I am one of innumerable humans.
And yet I am treasured enough to be summoned by name.
I am in Christ.
Christ is in me.
And I am hidden with Christ in God.
That means the One who holds the galaxies also speaks my name
with intention.
He calls me into this moment.
And this one.
And this one.
Nothing about my life is random to Him.
The darkness doesn't disqualify me.

It may very well be the place where He hides the treasure.
And the treasure isn't just resilience.
It isn't just maturity.
It isn't just spiritual depth.
The treasure is knowing Him more fully — the One who calls me
by name.

Reflective Question
Where in my current season might God be hiding a treasure —
and am I willing to trust that even here, in this specific moment,
He is calling me by name into something deeper?

Prayer
Father,
It overwhelms me that You call me by name.
Not as a number.
Not as a face in a crowd.
Not as one more believer in a long line of believers.
You know me.
You see me.

You speak my name with purpose.

If there are treasures hidden in this season — even in places that feel dark — help me not to run from them. Help me to walk with You through them. Help me to trust that You are not wasting anything.

Thank You that You don't diminish who I am. Thank You that You use exactly who You made me to be. Thank You that I am not lost in the masses, but personally called, personally known, personally treasured.

Keep calling me into more.

Call me out of fear.

Call me out of distraction.

Call me out of lesser things.

And when You speak my name, help me to answer.

I'm Yours.

Amen

Rabbit Trail 12 — Still His People

Scripture

Genesis 12:1–3

Exodus 6:6–7

Deuteronomy 7:7–8

There are days I recognize myself in the Israelites far more than I'd like to admit.

They were God's chosen people—clearly and unmistakably. God cut covenant with Abraham and made promises that had nothing to do with Abraham's perfection and everything to do with God's faithfulness.

Those promises didn't stall out with time. They actually multiplied. Abraham's family grew into a people so numerous, so visibly blessed, that even a powerful Pharaoh felt threatened by them. He may not have known he was witnessing the fulfillment of God's promise, but he knew enough to fear what he was seeing. And Pharoah's fear led to the Israelites' oppression.

But even in slavery, God's people continued to multiply. Even in bondage, His blessing could not be extinguished.

Eventually, God called Moses, equipped him, and brought His people out of Egypt with unmistakable power—provision, protection, direction, and presence marked every step into freedom and promise.

And yet... the Israelites grumbled.

They doubted.

They grew impatient.

They longed for what was familiar instead of trusting what God promised.

They questioned God's goodness and resisted the leaders He had placed among them for their own good.

And still—they were His people. Period.

Their behavior wavered greatly, but their identity never did.

Their obedience miserably faltered, but God's covenant stood soundly.

When I sit with that truth, it steadies me.

Because there are days I am rescued and still restless. There are days I am provided for and still dissatisfied. There are days I know God is faithful, yet I still struggle to trust Him with the pace or the process.

I can become impatient. I can wander. I can grumble quietly—or not so quietly—when the road feels long and the answers feel slow.

And yet... my identity does not dissolve in those moments.

I am STILL His child.

My Father is STILL the King.

My Father is STILL the Creator of all things.

My Father is STILL God—God above all gods.

Israel's wilderness wandering did not mean they were no longer chosen. It meant they had forgotten who they were. The tragedy wasn't simply their disobedience—it was their forgetfulness. If they had remembered whose they were, they might not have spent so long walking in circles in the wilderness.

This comforts me more than it excuses me.
Because it assures me that remembering my identity doesn't remove responsibility—it restores direction. When I remember who I am and whose I am, my steps grow steadier. My heart softens. My impatience loosens its grip.
I don't want to live as though my failures redefine me. I want to live as someone marked by covenant, not performance. I want to live grounded, not frantic. I want to live held, not abandoned.
Even when I wander—even when I am childish or frustrated or spiritually pitching a fit—I am STILL His.
And remembering that changes everything for me.

Reflective Question
Where in my life am I tempted to believe that my frustration, impatience, or confusion has altered who I am to God—and what might change if I allowed Him to remind me that I am still His?

Prayer

Father,

I come to You just as I am—tired, imperfect, sometimes impatient, sometimes unsure.

I crawl close and rest in You, asking You to let me see myself through Your eyes.

Remind me who I am when I forget. Remind me whose I am when I wander.

Pour Your grace over me, especially in the places where I struggle to extend grace to myself.

Shape my heart to look more like Christ—not through striving, but through nearness.

Hold me steady in Your truth, and let Your love quiet every fear.

Amen

Rabbit Trail 13 — Loved, Even When Rejected
1 John 3:1 (NLT)
See how very much our Father loves us, for He calls us His children, and that is what we are! But the people who belong to this world don't recognize that we are God's children because they don't know Him.
That verse steadies me.
He calls us His children, and that is what we are.
Before it says anything about misunderstanding.
Before it mentions not being recognized.
Before it addresses rejection.
It anchors identity first.
And then it tells the truth:
Some won't recognize us.
Because they don't know Him.
There have been moments when I have felt misunderstood simply because I am carrying Christ. Moments when kindness was met with suspicion. When conviction was labeled judgment. When surrender looked strange. When choosing not to participate in something felt like quiet rebellion to someone else.
It's tempting in those moments to take it personally.
But Jesus didn't leave us guessing about this.
John 15:18–19 (NLT)
"If the world hates you, remember that it hated me first. The world would love you as one of its own if you belonged to it, but you are no longer part of the world. I chose you to come out of the world, so it hates you."

He says this calmly. Not dramatically. Not bitterly. Just clearly.
If I am imaging Him accurately — if I am carrying His Spirit —
then it is only reasonable to expect that those who reject Him
may resist me too.
That doesn't mean I'm doing something wrong.
It may mean I am reflecting Him honestly.
And then there is this — words that are hard, but somehow
comforting:
Matthew 5:10–12 (NLT)
God blesses those who are persecuted for doing right,
for the Kingdom of Heaven is theirs.
"God blesses you when people mock you and persecute you and lie
about you and say all sorts of evil things against you because you
are my followers. Rejoice and be glad! For a great reward awaits
you in heaven. And remember, the ancient prophets were
persecuted in the same way."
Blessed?
That's not how it feels in the moment.
But what He is saying is this: when rejection comes because you
are following Me, you are standing in the company of prophets.
You are standing in alignment with truth. You are not outside My
will — you are in it.
Rejection does not cancel belonging.
It may confirm it.
And yet — this is important — I don't want to become
hardened.

I don't want to wear rejection like a badge and grow defensive. I don't want to expect hostility everywhere and live guarded.
Because the goal is not to win arguments.
It's to image Him.
If someone's picture of God has been distorted — if they've only seen harshness, manipulation, or hypocrisy — then my job is not to shame them for that.
My job is to reflect who He truly is:
Utter kindness.
Pure mercy.
Provision without strings.
Truth without cruelty.
Holiness without pride.
If they reject Him, and I am carrying Him, then yes — they may reject me.
But if they ever see Him clearly — through patience, through consistency, through real love — their guard may fall.
Not because I forced it.
But because love stayed steady.
And underneath all of it, this remains true:
He calls us His children — and that is what we are.
Whether the world recognizes it or not.

Reflective Question
When I feel misunderstood or rejected because of my faith, do I
shrink back, grow defensive, or become bitter — or do I
remember whose image I carry and respond with the same
steady kindness Christ has shown me?

Prayer
Father,
Thank You for calling me Your child.
When rejection stings, help me remember who I belong to. When I
feel misunderstood, remind me that You were misunderstood first.
Guard my heart from pride and from bitterness. I don't want to
become hardened. I want to reflect You accurately — Your
kindness, Your patience, Your mercy.
If someone resists me because I carry You, help me respond with
grace instead of defense.
Let my life soften what has been hardened by misrepresentation.
And when it's hard, steady me with this truth:
I am Your child.
And that is enough.
Amen

Rabbit Trail 14 — Adopted, Not Orphaned

Romans 8:15–17 (NLT)

So you have not received a spirit that makes you fearful slaves. Instead, you received God's Spirit when he adopted you as his own children. Now we call him, "Abba, Father."

For his Spirit joins with our spirit to affirm that we are God's children.

And since we are his children, we are his heirs. In fact, together with Christ we are heirs of God's glory. But if we are to share his glory, we must also share his suffering.

There was a time when I lived like an orphan and didn't even know it.

Before I understood His love — or maybe before I allowed my heart to actually receive it — I was enslaved to fear. Not necessarily trembling fear all the time, but that underlying pressure that says:

Secure yourself.

Prove yourself.

Protect yourself.

Provide for yourself.

Don't trust too much.

That is slavery.

When we walk in the flesh, we make decisions based on self-preservation. Financial security becomes god. Appearance becomes god. Status becomes god. Education becomes god. Possessions become god. Even "being right" can become god.

And whatever becomes god becomes master.

You cannot serve two masters.

When I am enslaved to the flesh — when my ambitions and insecurities dictate my choices — I may feel powerful in moments, but underneath it, there is always anxiety. Always striving. Always fear of losing what I've clung to.

Because idols demand.

They never satisfy.

Meanwhile, the inner man is starving for God.

The hunger is real.

And when we try to fill that hunger with something else, we become slaves to that substitute.

But Romans says we have not received a spirit of fearful slavery.

We have received adoption.

Adoption changes everything.

An orphan survives.

A son rests.

An orphan hustles for belonging.

A daughter already belongs.

An orphan fears abandonment.

A child calls out, "Abba."

Abba is intimate. It's not formal. It's not distant. It's not "Most High Authority Figure." It's relational.

And here's what amazes me: surrendering to Him looks like losing control, but it actually lightens the burden.

When I was enslaved to the flesh, the burden was heavy. Every decision carried the weight of securing my own significance.

But when I surrender to Christ, His yoke is easy and His burden is light.

Yes, there is suffering. The verse says we share in His glory —
and we also share in His suffering. There will be pushback. There
will be misunderstanding. There will be exclusion at times.
But that suffering is not the crushing weight of self-made
identity.
It is the refining fire of belonging.
When I became His child, I didn't just receive protection and
provision — I received inheritance.
Heir.
That means I don't work to earn a place in the family.
I already have one.
And here's the beautiful, steady truth: His Spirit affirms it. There
is an inner witness. Something in me that resonates when I call
Him Father.
Before adoption, surrender felt terrifying.
To take on His name.
To fall under His rule.
To entrust Him with my well-being.
That feels risky.
But once I surrendered, I realized something:
Everything I was chasing was found there.
Security.
Identity.
Provision.
Love without manipulation.
Correction without rejection.
Adopted.
Not orphaned.

And even when life feels painful — even when I'm misunderstood or walking through hard seasons — I am covered. I am provided for. I am treasured.

I am not surviving alone.

I am His.

And here's the part that steadies me in a way almost nothing else can.

Colossians 3:3–4 (NLT)

For you died to this life, and your real life is hidden with Christ in God.

And when Christ, who is your life, is revealed to the whole world, you will share in all his glory.

My real life is hidden.

Hidden with Christ.

In God.

Just let that settle.

If I am adopted, then I am His child.

If I am His child, then I am an heir.

If I am an heir, then my inheritance is not fragile.

And if my life is hidden with Christ in God, then it is secure beyond anything this world can shake.

Before adoption, I lived like an orphan — protecting, striving, clinging, hustling for security.

Now?

Now I am layered in belonging.

I am in Christ.

Christ is in me.

And Christ is in God.

That means my identity isn't hanging out in the open for the world to define.

It isn't vulnerable to every opinion.

It isn't up for renegotiation when I fail or when someone misunderstands me.

It is hidden.

Secured.

Held.

And here's what humbles me most:

This isn't just about comfort.

It's about purpose.

As an heir, I don't just inherit safety — I inherit participation.

Christ in me means divine life is actively at work inside me.

Me in Christ means I am positioned in Him, not scrambling to build my own significance.

Hidden with Christ in God means even when I can't see what He's doing, even when the path feels unclear, I am not wandering.

We are walking something eternal.

Together.

Not because I earned it.

But because I was adopted into it.

Not orphaned.

Adopted.

Not striving alone.

Hidden, secure, and included in divine purpose.

Reflective Question

If my real life is truly hidden with Christ in God — secure, adopted, and positioned as an heir — where am I still living as though I have to protect, prove, or secure myself instead of resting in that belonging and walking confidently in shared purpose?

Prayer

Dad,

Sometimes I forget I'm not an orphan anymore.

Sometimes I still grip things like it's all up to me. I still try to secure what You've already promised. I still hustle for safety when You've already wrapped my life in Yours.

But when I read that my real life is hidden with Christ in You...

it quiets me.

That means I'm safe.

That means I'm seen.

That means I'm not exposed or fragile or left out in the cold.

I am in Christ.

Christ is in me.

And my life is held inside You.

That's more security than I even know how to process.

Thank You for adopting me. Thank You for not leaving me to survive on my own instincts. Thank You that surrender didn't increase my burden — it lifted it.

Teach me to live like a daughter.

Teach me to rest like an heir.

Teach me to walk in the purpose You've woven around and through
my life — not anxiously, not fearfully — but confidently,
because I belong.
I'm so grateful I get to call You Abba.
And even more grateful that You call me Yours.
Amen

Rabbit Trail 15 — Treasured and Made New
1 Peter 2:9
But you are a chosen race, a royal priesthood, a holy nation, a people for God's own possession, so that you may proclaim the excellencies of Him who called you out of darkness into His marvelous light.
2 Corinthians 5:17
Therefore, if anyone is in Christ, he is a new creation. The old has passed away; behold, the new has come.
There is something breathtaking about those two truths sitting side by side.
I am God's treasured possession.
And I am a new creation.
Not patched up.
Not slightly improved.
New.
When I surrendered my life to Christ — not just asking Him to rescue me from consequences, but actually inviting Him to be Lord — something fundamental shifted. I didn't become a slightly shinier version of the old me. I became new.
That doesn't mean I don't remember the rust.
It doesn't mean I don't recognize the places that were weathered and worn. But it does mean that the old identity — the one defined by fear, shame, failure, inconsistency — is not the truest version of me anymore.

The old has passed away.
The new has come.
And here's where it ties so deeply into being His treasured possession:
God does not treasure junk.
He restores.
He renews.
He makes new.
I think about that old wood stove that sat outside for years. It still had the ability to burn. It was still built for heat and warmth. But it wasn't functioning as designed. It was rusted. It was packed with ash. It looked unusable.
When my brother restored it, he didn't just admire it as it was. He cleaned it. Reconnected it. Refitted it. And when it burned again, it wasn't pretending to be something new — it was operating as it was always intended to.
That's what God does with me.
He doesn't call me His treasured possession while leaving me corroded and disconnected.
He restores.
He recreates.
He breathes life into what sin distorted.
And because I am His treasured possession, He doesn't treat my transformation casually.
He is intentional.
Being "new" doesn't mean I erase my history.
It means my history no longer defines my identity.
Being His treasured possession doesn't mean I'm stored away.

It means I'm set apart, cherished, and actively being shaped for His purpose.

I am in Christ.

Christ is in me.

The broken image handed down from the garden does not get the final word. Through surrender, through sanctification, through daily walking with Him, He restores an accurate reflection of Himself in me.

That is both humbling and exhilarating.

He treasures me enough to make me new.

And He makes me new so that I can proclaim His excellencies — so that my life becomes evidence of what restoration looks like.

Not perfection.

Restoration.

And every time I forget who I am, every time I start identifying more with the rust than the renewal, I can come back to this:

I am His.

And I am new.

Reflective Question

Where in my life am I still identifying with the "old" version of myself — the rust, the failure, the shame — instead of living from the truth that I am God's treasured possession and a new creation in Christ?

Prayer

Father,

You didn't just save me.

You made me new.

Thank You for not treasuring a broken version of me while leaving me that way. Thank You for restoring, reconnecting, renewing. Sometimes I still feel like that old stove sitting on the porch — weathered and worn. And yet You see something different. You see what You created me to be. You see what You're making me into.

Help me stop clinging to the old identity.

Help me stop rehearsing who I was instead of walking in who I am.

I am Yours.

I am treasured.

And in Christ, I am new.

Keep refining me. Keep restoring me. Keep burning brightly through me so that my life proclaims how good You are.

I love You.

Amen

Rabbit Trail 16 — No Longer I
Galatians 2:20
"I have been crucified with Christ. It is no longer I who live, but Christ who lives in me. And the life I now live in the flesh I live by faith in the Son of God, who loved me and gave himself for me."

There are times when I read Scripture and realize that the words "no longer I" are far more unsettling than they are comforting. They ask me to consider how many versions of myself I've tried to live from—some formed by circumstance, some by fear, some by reaction, some by survival.
Moses comes to mind.
His life began under a death sentence. Before he ever had a chance to know who he was, someone else had already decided he should not exist. He was hidden, placed in a basket, set afloat—his survival dependent entirely on God's unseen hand. And the one who drew him out of the water did not know his true identity. He was raised in a palace by the very people who would one day enslave his own.
Born a Hebrew.
Raised as royalty.
Too Hebrew to belong fully to Egypt.
Too Egyptian to be trusted by his people.
I can't imagine how many times Moses must have wondered who he really was. Which story defined him? Which name fit? Which world claimed him?

Rabbit Trail 16 — No Longer I
Galatians 2:20
"I have been crucified with Christ. It is no longer I who live, but Christ who lives in me. And the life I now live in the flesh I live by faith in the Son of God, who loved me and gave himself for me."

There are times when I read Scripture and realize that the words "no longer I" are far more unsettling than they are comforting. They ask me to consider how many versions of myself I've tried to live from—some formed by circumstance, some by fear, some by reaction, some by survival.
Moses comes to mind.
His life began under a death sentence. Before he ever had a chance to know who he was, someone else had already decided he should not exist. He was hidden, placed in a basket, set afloat—his survival dependent entirely on God's unseen hand. And the one who drew him out of the water did not know his true identity. He was raised in a palace by the very people who would one day enslave his own.
Born a Hebrew.
Raised as royalty.
Too Hebrew to belong fully to Egypt.
Too Egyptian to be trusted by his people.
I can't imagine how many times Moses must have wondered who he really was. Which story defined him? Which name fit? Which world claimed him?

Reflective Question

As I sit with God, where might He be gently inviting me to release a version of myself shaped by reaction, fear, or circumstance— so that I can more fully live from Christ in me and trust His redemptive purpose in every part of my story?

Prayer

Father,

I come to You with all the versions of myself I've tried to live from—the ones shaped by fear, confusion, and survival. I lay them down before You. Teach me what it means to say, "no longer I," not with loss, but with trust. Let Christ live fully in me. Help me believe that no season has been wasted and no part of my story is beyond Your redemption. Lead me out of reaction and into obedience, out of striving and into surrender. I place my life —every chapter, every question—back into Your hands, confident that You are still writing something good.

Amen

Rabbit Trail 17 — Carriers of the Flame
John 15:5 (NLT)
"Yes, I am the vine; you are the branches. Those who remain in me, and I in them, will produce much fruit. For apart from me you can do nothing."

I was lighting candles the other day. A couple dozen of them. Not with a torch — just a simple wooden match.
And something small but telling kept happening.
If I held the lit match just close enough to the wick — with a little space between them — the wick would catch beautifully. The flame would transfer without strain. The candle would come alive.
But when I got impatient — when I pressed the match directly against the wick, thinking that closer meant faster — the opposite happened. The flame on the match would suffocate. It couldn't breathe. It would go out before the wick ever caught fire.
Too close didn't help.
It hindered.
And I couldn't help but see myself in that moment.
When I am excited about what God is doing — when I feel lit up, passionate, alive — I want the people around me to feel that too.
I want them to catch it. I want them to burn bright with the same joy.

But sometimes, in my exuberance, I get too close. I press. I crowd.
I assume that if I just hold the flame right up against them long
enough, they'll ignite.
And instead of lighting them, I risk suffocating myself.
I forget something important.
I carry the flame.
I am not the source of the flame.
Jesus said, "I am the vine; you are the branches." Not the vine.
Not the source. Not the origin of life. Just the branch — fully
dependent, fully supplied.
When I try to act like the source — when I try to manufacture
ignition in someone else — I exhaust myself. I feel wounded when
they don't "catch." I feel diminished when my passion isn't
mirrored. I forget that fruit grows from abiding, not from
pressure.
God's flame cannot be extinguished. His fire does not suffocate.
He can handle any level of closeness without being diminished. His
light is self-sustaining.
Mine is not.
And that is not a weakness — it is design.
I was never created to be the source. I was created to bear the
flame, to carry it faithfully, to share it wisely, to respect the
space and timing of others, and to trust that God is the one who
ignites hearts.
When I remember that, everything steadies.
I can burn brightly without forcing.
I can share without crowding.

I can give space without feeling rejected.
Because my identity is not "the fire starter."
My identity is "the branch that abides."
Christ in me.
Me in Christ.
The life flows from Him. The warmth flows through me.
And when I stay rooted — when I remain — fruit happens naturally. Not because I pressed harder, but because I stayed connected.
That is freeing.

Reflective Question
Where in my life might I be trying to act as the source instead of the carrier — and how would my relationships, my passion, and my peace shift if I trusted God to ignite what only He can ignite?

Prayer

Father,

Thank You that I do not have to be the source. Thank You that the flame was never mine to manufacture or sustain. Forgive me for the times I have pressed too hard, tried to control outcomes, or felt wounded when others did not respond the way I hoped. Teach me to abide. Keep me rooted in You. Let the life that flows through me be gentle, steady, and true. Help me carry Your flame with humility and wisdom, trusting You to light what You choose to light. I am grateful to be a branch in Your vine — supplied, sustained, and secure.

Amen

Rabbit Trail 18 — Not by Lineage, but by Surrender

Genesis 14:18–20; Hebrews 7:3; Psalm 110:4

There are places in Scripture where God seems to pause the narrative just long enough to say, Pay attention. This matters. Melchizedek is one of those pauses.

In Genesis 14, after Abraham rescues Lot, two kings come out to meet him. One wants to take. The other wants to bless.

And into that moment steps this mysterious royal priest:

Genesis 14:18–20 (NLT)

And Melchizedek, the king of Salem and a priest of God Most High, brought Abram some bread and wine. Melchizedek blessed Abram with this blessing:

"Blessed be Abram by God Most High,

Creator of heaven and earth.

And blessed be God Most High,

who has defeated your enemies for you."

Then Abram gave Melchizedek a tenth of all the goods he had recovered.

No genealogy.

No background story.

No tribe listed.

No explanation.

Just this: king. priest. surrendered to God Most High.

Later, Hebrews reflects back and says something astonishing:
Hebrews 7:3 (NLT)
There is no record of his father or mother or any of his ancestors—no beginning or end to his life. He remains a priest forever, resembling the Son of God.
It doesn't say he didn't have parents. It says they're not the point.
His authority did not rest on lineage.
His significance did not rest on documentation.
His priesthood did not require a human stamp of approval.
God honored him because he was surrendered — a conduit between heaven and earth.
And then Psalm 110 speaks prophetically of the coming Messiah:
Psalm 110:4 (NLT)
The Lord has taken an oath and will not break his vow: "You are a priest forever in the order of Melchizedek."
Jesus Himself — not from the tribe of Levi, not from the priestly line — is declared a priest forever through a higher order.
Not by lineage.
By divine appointment.
And here is where the rabbit trail circles back to identity.
When I am in Christ and Christ is in me, I share in that royal priesthood. Not because of who my ancestors were. Not because of my resume. Not because someone validated me.
But because I am surrendered to the God of all gods.
Melchizedek reminds me that humans do not get to define God's order.

Men record genealogies.
God establishes priesthood.
Men value pedigree.
God values surrender.
Men look for credentials.
God looks for availability.
If Melchizedek's beginning wasn't recorded and his end wasn't recorded, yet he stands as a royal priest honored by Scripture itself, then my worth is not anchored to my backstory either.
My beginning does not determine my authority.
My past does not determine my priesthood.
My failures do not cancel my calling.
What determines it?
Surrender.
When I remain surrendered, I become a conduit — not a source, not a performer, not a personality — but a conduit.
A clean straw through which heaven flows into earth.
A royal priest does two things:
Represents God to humanity.
Represents humanity to God.
That is identity.
That is responsibility.
That is privilege.

And it does not require applause.

It requires surrender.

When I allow shame, pride, insecurity, or performance to clog that conduit, I am still loved — but I am less clear. Less free. Less usable.

But when I come before Him and say, "Clean the straw," when I choose surrender over self-definition, He clears the pathway again.

I don't have to manufacture authority.

I don't have to demand validation.

I don't have to secure a title.

In Christ, I am royal priesthood — not because of lineage, but because of surrender.

And in every moment of my life, whether visible or hidden, God's eternal purposes are flowing through that surrendered connection.

That is who I am.

Reflective Question

Where am I still seeking validation from human lineage, approval, or recognition instead of resting in the authority that comes from simple, wholehearted surrender to God? Is there anything clogging the conduit?

Prayer

Father God,

You are the One who establishes identity. You are the One who assigns authority. You are the One who sees what men overlook. Thank You that my worth is not determined by my backstory, my credentials, my failures, or my visibility. Thank You that in Christ, I am part of a royal priesthood — not by pedigree, but by surrender.

Search me. Clean anything in me that blocks Your flow. Remove pride. Remove insecurity. Remove shame. Remove the need to be seen.

Make me a clear conduit — a willing, joyful connection between heaven and earth.

Let Your heart move through me.

Let Your grace move through me.

Let Your power move through me.

And remind me again and again that my identity is secure — not because men recognize it, but because You declared it.

I am Yours.

You are mine.

And Your purposes are flowing even now.

Amen

Rabbit Trail 19 — Not Condemned

Romans 8:1 (NLT)

So now there is no condemnation for those who belong to Christ Jesus.

That is not a small sentence.

That is not just a comforting thought.

That is radical freedom.

And it goes far beyond simply being "forgiven."

Romans 8 is not about barely escaping judgment. It's not about being saved from the fire and then sitting safely on the sidelines. It's about living as a new creation — empowered, transformed, aligned with the Spirit.

"No condemnation" is the doorway.

Transformation is the life beyond it.

Before I knew Him — or before I was willing to believe that what He did was enough — my identity was confusing. I was conflicted. Pulled by the flesh. Enslaved to impulses, fear, pride, insecurity. I thought I knew truth, but I only had fragments gathered from the natural world around me.

And that tainted image shaped how I saw myself.

Then I heard the good news.

Christ was who He said He was.

He did what He said He would do.

He shed His blood so that I could be forgiven, restored, reconciled.

And when I believed that — when I received it — something immediate happened.
Justified.
Not "on probation."
Not "almost accepted."
Not "conditionally tolerated."
Justified.
God no longer holds my sin against me.
That doesn't mean there isn't transformation ahead. There absolutely is. But the transformation is not me earning approval. It is me allowing Him to align me with what I already am in Christ.
No condemnation is not based on my feelings.
It is not based on how hard I am on myself.
It is not based on whether I condemn myself first so that maybe God won't.
It is based solely on Christ's righteousness.
That means my standing is secure.
And that changes everything.
When I am in Christ, I walk according to the Spirit, not the flesh.
I am clothed in Him. The penalty is gone. The shame is gone. The eternal consequence is gone.
And this freedom is my birthright as someone born again.
Radical freedom.
I think about prodigals.

Have you ever watched someone you love — deeply love — make destructive choices? Choices that hurt themselves and everyone around them? And you, and everyone else who loves them, longs for nothing more than to pull them in close and wrap them in reassurance?

You see their value.

You see their potential.

You see their worth.

But they only see their guilt.

So they beat themselves up.

And in doing so, they push away the very arms that long to hold them.

That's what condemnation does.

It keeps us from receiving what is already being offered.

God is not standing at a distance waiting for us to grovel correctly.

He already gave everything so we could be restored.

"No condemnation" means the door is open.

It means the Father is not rehearsing your failures.

It means you have passed from death into life.

It means when He sees you, He sees Christ's righteousness covering you.

And from that secure standing — not from fear — transformation begins.

He does the work.
We surrender.
He aligns.
We respond.
He sanctifies.
We trust.
The goal isn't just to be pardoned.
The goal is to be transformed from the fallen, tainted image into a purer reflection of Christ. Not by striving. Not by self-punishment. Not by fear of disappointing Him.
But by love.
When I see myself the way He sees me — welcomed, justified, adopted, treasured — it shrinks the negative thoughts. It puts my failures in perspective. It dismantles the lie that says I am cast off.
Condemnation says, "You are your worst moment."
The gospel says, "You are Mine."
And when that finally sinks in — when I truly see myself through His eyes — gratitude floods in.
Not because I deserve it.
But because He chose to give it.

Reflective Question
Am I still relating to God from a place of self-condemnation — trying to earn what has already been secured — or am I living from the freedom of knowing there is truly no condemnation for me in Christ?

Prayer

Father,

Your Word says You remove my sins as far as the east is from the west.

That means they are gone.

Not hidden.

Not tucked away somewhere.

Gone.

And yet sometimes I still carry them.

Sometimes I replay mistakes You have already forgiven.

Sometimes I hold myself to a judgment You have already lifted.

Forgive me for trying to hold onto what You have already dissolved.

Help me see myself the way You see me.

If the blood of Christ has covered my sin, teach my heart to stop uncovering it. If You have removed it, teach my mind to stop searching for it.

Let Your forgiveness wash over me the way that water dissolves rice paper — until there is nothing left to cling to me.

Thank You that You did not forgive me reluctantly.

You wanted to restore me.

You made a way for me to come home.

You welcome me fully.

Help me walk in that freedom.

Help me see myself through Your eyes — completely forgiven, completely loved, and secure in Christ.

Amen

Rabbit Trail 20 — Fully Forgiven
Psalm 103:12 (NLT)
He has removed our sins as far from us
as the east is from the west.
That is an immeasurable distance.
If the verse had said north from south, eventually you would
reach a pole. But east and west never meet. You can travel east
forever and never reach west.
That is the distance God places between me and my sin when He
forgives me.
Completely removed.
Not tucked away.
Not set aside for later discussion.
Removed.
And yet, if I'm honest, something inside me still wrestles with that.
God forgives me — fully, completely — but sometimes I struggle
to forgive myself.
Why is that?
If the God who sees absolutely everything about me — every
motive, every failure, every hidden thought — if He is willing to
forgive me completely through the sacrifice of Christ, what is it in
me that still holds onto condemnation?
If I look closely, I think it has to be pride.
Because when I refuse to accept His forgiveness, what I'm really
saying is:
"God, You may forgive me... but I won't."
That means I'm placing my judgment above His.

In a subtle way, it's like trying to crawl up into His throne and say that my verdict should carry more weight than His mercy.
That realization is humbling.
Because forgiveness was never something I could manufacture. I didn't earn it. I didn't clean myself up enough to deserve it. Christ spilled His blood so that forgiveness could be complete.
There is nothing the blood of Christ does not cover.
Not my worst moment.
Not my deepest regret.
Not the thing I wish I could undo.
All of it.
Covered.
Removed.
But learning to see myself the way God sees me — fully forgiven — can be a process. My mind wants to replay the mistake. My heart wants to rehearse the regret. Shame whispers that maybe I should carry it just a little longer.
As if dragging it behind me somehow honors God.
But it doesn't.
It only distorts my identity.
Because if I am in Christ, and Christ is in me, then my identity is not "the person who failed." My identity is "the person who has been forgiven and restored."

Refusing to release my own condemnation keeps me from walking freely in that truth.

It doesn't change how God sees me.

But it changes how I see myself. That is important, as it influences how I walk through this life.

There were times when I found myself praying about something I said I was trusting God with — something deeply important — yet I would keep taking it back. I would carry the weight of it again, worrying about how it would be answered or when it would be answered. I realized sometimes my heart needed something tangible to help me release what I had given to Him.

So I would write the prayer request on a thin piece of rice paper and stir it into water.

The paper would dissolve.

The words would disappear.

I couldn't retrieve it. I couldn't gather it back up again. It was simply gone.

That little act became a picture for me of what it means to release something to God and leave it there.

Sometimes I think forgiveness could be practiced the same way. Imagine writing down every failure you struggle to forgive yourself for — every regret, every moment that still nags at your heart — and stirring that rice paper into a vat of warm water until it dissolves completely.

Gone.

Now imagine stepping down into that water.

You dunk down under the surface and come back up.
You might expect that all those failures are still clinging to you
— that anyone who looks at you could read them written all
over you.
But if someone standing nearby were asked to list all the failures
they see on you, they would say:
"I see nothing."
There's nothing written on you.
Nothing clinging to you.
All they would see is water.
You could dunk down into that water fifty times and come back
up fifty times, and no matter how carefully someone looked at
you, they still would not see those failures.
They were dissolved.
Removed.
Gone.
And sometimes I've thought about baptism in a similar way.
I've often wished that when we were baptized, the water could
somehow be scarlet — the color of Christ's sacrifice.
That I could step into the water looking like myself, carrying all
my imperfections, all the things that once defined me... and then
go under.
And when I came back up, everything visible would be scarlet.
My hair dripping scarlet.
My skin covered in scarlet.
Every drop running down me the color of Christ's blood.

Not because I am stained by sin — but because I am covered by His sacrifice.

It would be such a powerful picture.

Because when God looks at me, He does not see the list of failures my mind still rehearses.

He sees the covering of Christ.

He sees the righteousness of His Son wrapped around me.

My sin has been removed.

My identity has been restored.

And the freedom He offers is real.

What God has dissolved in His mercy, I must stop trying to recover with my memory.

Reflective Question

If God has truly dissolved my sins and removed them as far as the east is from the west, what would change in the way I see myself if I stopped searching for failures that He has already erased?

Is there something I keep holding against myself that God has already removed?

Father,
Your Word says You remove my sins as far as the east is from the west.
That means they are gone.
Not hidden.
Not tucked away somewhere.
Gone.
And yet sometimes I still carry them.
Sometimes I replay mistakes You have already forgiven.
Sometimes I hold myself to a judgment You have already lifted.
Forgive me for trying to hold onto what You have already dissolved.
Help me see myself the way You see me.
If the blood of Christ has covered my sin, teach my heart to stop uncovering it. If You have removed it, teach my mind to stop searching for it.
Let Your forgiveness wash over me the way water dissolves rice paper — until there is nothing left to cling to me.
And remind me that when You look at me, You do not see my failures. You see the covering of Christ.
Thank You that You did not forgive me reluctantly.
You wanted to restore me.
You made a way for me to come home.
You welcome me fully.
Help me walk in that freedom.
Help me see myself through Your eyes — completely forgiven, completely loved, and secure in Christ.
Amen

Rabbit Trail 21 — God's Workmanship
Ephesians 2:10 (AMP)
For we are His workmanship [His own master work, a work of art], created in Christ Jesus [reborn from above—spiritually transformed, renewed, ready to be used] for good works, which God prepared [for us] beforehand [taking paths which He set], so that we would walk in them [living the good life which He prearranged and made ready for us].

This verse makes me pause every time I read it.

I am His workmanship.

Not something mass-produced.

Not something accidental.

Not something hurried.

A master work.

A work of art.

When someone creates something meaningful, they don't do it casually. They enter into a space intentionally. They set aside distractions. They gather the materials. Their focus becomes the work in front of them.

I think about the spaces where I create things. When I work with pottery, for example, there's a place for it. Everything I need is there. I step into that space and the rest of the world fades into the background. My hands are focused on shaping what's in front of me.

And when I read this verse, I imagine something similar — except the space God entered was Christ Jesus.

I was created in Christ Jesus.
It's as if God stepped into that sacred space — Christ Himself
— and began shaping something new. And what He was shaping
was me.
Now, when I create something, I start with materials that already
exist. I take pieces and parts and begin combining them, altering
them, forming them into something new.
But God is able to do something even more remarkable.
He takes a life that already exists — with all its experiences,
mistakes, personality, history, and broken pieces — and through
Christ, He recreates it.
Reborn from above.
Spiritually transformed.
Renewed.
Not just improved.
Made new.
And then comes something that fills me with awe.
This transformation wasn't just for the sake of having converts
or followers.
God had good works prepared beforehand.
Before I was transformed...
Before I even understood who He was...
Before I was aware of the life He intended for me...
He had already prepared the paths.
Not random opportunities.
Prepared paths.

Prepared paths.

Paths He designed so that I could walk in them.

And those paths lead to good works — works that will not be finished until God Himself can look at them and say, "That is good."

And when we hear "good works," sometimes we immediately think of what people call ministry.

Preaching.

Teaching.

Singing.

Mission work.

But God's good works are often far more woven into the ordinary fabric of everyday life.

They happen in conversations.

In how we respond to people.

In the kindness we offer.

In the patience we choose.

In the way we love people who are difficult to love.

In the way we cover someone instead of exposing them.

In the way we offer help quietly when someone is struggling.

These everyday moments become the places where God's workmanship is visible.

Our lives become ministry.

Our lives become worship.

Everyone who belongs to Christ carries a beautiful purpose. Every believer has good works prepared for them. Every one of us has paths that God prepared long before we ever realized we were walking them.

And sometimes the way we image God is more visible than we realize.

I think about my own appearance sometimes. I have a very distinct nose — my dad's nose. When I look in the mirror, there's no denying whose daughter I am.

People who knew my parents sometimes recognize it immediately. "You must be Jim and Connie's daughter."

And that realization brings with it a quiet responsibility.

Because if people know who my parents are by looking at me... then the way I live reflects on them.

The way I speak.

The way I treat people.

The way I respond when things go wrong.

All of it carries their image.

And the same is true with my heavenly Father.

When I walk through the world, people should be able to sense whose daughter I am.

Not because I say it loudly.

But because they see His character reflected in my life.

In the way I love.

In the way I forgive.

In the way I extend grace.

In the way I respond when life is hard.

And when that happens, something beautiful occurs.

People begin to desire Him — not because of a speech I gave, but because they see His image reflected in my life.

I am in Christ.

Christ is in me.

And there is purpose in every single moment of my life.

Each day I pray that I will keep the divine appointments God places before me — that I will notice the people He places in my path and allow Him to orchestrate the ordinary moments of my day into something meaningful.

Because when God sets His attention on creating a masterpiece, He does not rush.

He works patiently.

Intentionally.

And without distraction.

And somehow, in His grace, that masterpiece is me.

Reflective Question

If I truly believe that I am God's workmanship — His carefully formed masterpiece created for good works — how might that change the way I approach the ordinary moments of my day? What might happen if I began each day expecting God to place divine appointments along my path?

Father,

It amazes me that You would call me Your workmanship.

A master work.

A work of art.

Sometimes when I look at myself, I see unfinished pieces. I see flaws. I see places where I wish I had responded better or loved better or trusted You more.

But You see something different.

You see the work You are still shaping.

Thank You for creating me in Christ Jesus and for transforming me into something new. Thank You that my life is not random — that You have prepared good works and meaningful paths for me to walk long before I even realized they were there.

Help me live today with open eyes and a willing heart.

Help me recognize the people You place in my path. Help me respond with Your kindness, Your patience, and Your grace so that when others encounter me, they catch a glimpse of You.

Let my life quietly reflect Your character.

And Father, continue shaping me into the masterpiece You intend me to be. Remove whatever does not reflect You and strengthen whatever does.

I trust Your hands.

And I'm grateful that You never stop working on the work of art You began.

Amen

Rabbit Trail 22 — A Royal Priesthood

1 Peter 2:9

But you are a chosen people, a royal priesthood, a holy nation, a people for God's own possession, so that you may proclaim the excellencies of Him who has called you out of darkness into His marvelous light.

There is so much contained in this one verse that it almost feels impossible to pass over it quickly.

God calls His people a royal priesthood.

That alone is staggering.

But then He also calls us a holy nation.

The Hebrew word for holy is kadosh. It means set apart, distinct, other than the ordinary. It means something separated from the common and dedicated completely to God.

The word is used for God Himself.

It is used for the temple.

It is used for the Sabbath.

And now it is used for His people.

If I am in Christ, and Christ is in me, and I am hidden with Christ in God, then I am part of that holy nation. That means my life is not meant to be shaped by the standards of the world around me.

The world does not get to decide what is good.

The world does not get to determine what is right.

The world does not get to redefine holiness.

Because the world's standard is not holy. It is altered. It is adjusted constantly to make room for sin, to justify desires, to normalize what God never called good.

If I measure myself by the world's standard, I will inevitably distort the temple of God.

And that temple is me.

Scripture tells us that believers are now the temple of God. His Spirit dwells within us. Which means if I allow the world to decide what is acceptable in my life, it is no different than when evil rulers in ancient times entered God's temple and replaced the worship of God with the worship of false gods.

They removed the sacred things.

They brought in idols.

They set up altars to something other than God.

And if I allow the world to determine how I should think, how I should speak, what I should celebrate, what I should tolerate, and what I should excuse, then the same thing happens within this temple.

The altar shifts.

The worship changes.

The presence is no longer honored.

But as a royal priest, my life is meant to be a connection point between heaven and earth.

Priests were always bridges between God and people.

They represented the people before God, and they represented God to the people.

That is still our calling.
I carry His Spirit.
I carry His presence.
I carry His image into the world around me.
And that will not always make people comfortable.
If people rejected Christ, it should not surprise me if they reject the image of Christ when they encounter it in me. If His words challenged people, it is only reasonable that His truth may challenge people through me as well.
But this is not about being harsh or arrogant.
In fact, the closer I walk with Him, the more humility grows in me.
Because the more clearly I see Him, the more clearly I see how far I fall short of His perfection.
Humility is not humiliation.
It is not shame.
It is not walking around feeling defeated.
Humility is simply seeing reality clearly.
It is recognizing the fullness of who God is and the overwhelming grace that allows me to stand in Him at all.
The more I see His holiness, the more I understand His mercy.
The more I see His perfection, the more grateful I become for His patience.
And the result is not pride.
It is awe.

And there is something else I've noticed about light.
Sometimes when I am working on a project late in the day, I become so absorbed in what I am doing that I don't realize how much time has passed. The daylight slowly fades, and the room grows darker and darker around me. But because it happens gradually, I don't notice it.
I keep working, thinking I can still see just fine.
It isn't until someone walks in and flips the light switch that I suddenly realize how dark the room had actually become.
All at once I can see clearly again — and I also see how blurred the details of my work had become in the dim light. I realize that what I thought I could see clearly was actually dim and shadowed.
It amazes me that darkness can grow that deep without my awareness.
And I never want that to be true of my life.
I never want darkness to creep in so gradually that I fail to notice it.
I never want my vision to become so dim that I start shaping my life in poor light — thinking I can see clearly when in reality the details are blurred.
Because when light is present, everything is revealed.
Light sharpens the details.
Light exposes what doesn't belong.
Light helps the work turn out the way it was meant to.
And that is exactly what God has done for us.
He has called us out of darkness into His marvelous light.

The purpose of being a chosen people, a royal priesthood, a holy nation is that our lives would declare His excellence.
If I continue to live like the darkness, justify the darkness, sound like the darkness, and celebrate the darkness, then how will anyone ever see the difference?
How will anyone be drawn to the light if my life looks exactly like the shadows they are already living in?
The point is not to separate myself from people.
The point is to love them enough to remain faithful to the truth that can bring them life.
Real love does not compromise truth in order to keep temporary peace.
Real love remains faithful to what leads people into light.
And when we walk in humility, kindness, truth, and grace, something powerful happens.
People begin to see glimpses of God.
Not because we are perfect.
But because we carry Him.
And sometimes the most loving thing we can do for the people around us is to faithfully reflect Him — even when that reflection makes them uncomfortable at first.
Because light always feels uncomfortable to eyes that have grown used to darkness.
But eventually, light reveals beauty that darkness never could.
And that is the calling of a royal priesthood.
To carry the light faithfully.
With humility.
With love.

And with the quiet confidence that the One whose image we bear
is worth it.

Reflective Question
Where in my life might darkness have slowly crept in without my
awareness?
What would it look like for me to intentionally keep God's light
shining on every area of my life so that I can reflect Him clearly
to the world around me?

Prayer

Father,

Thank You for calling me out of darkness into Your marvelous light. There were places in my life where I could not see clearly until Your light shined on them. Even now, I know there are places where I still need Your light to reveal what I cannot see on my own.

Keep my heart sensitive to You.

Do not allow darkness to slowly creep in where I become comfortable with things that do not reflect Your holiness.

Let Your light continually shine on my life so that what You are shaping in me can be formed clearly and beautifully according to Your design.

Help me walk as part of Your royal priesthood with humility and love. Let the way I speak, the way I live, and the way I love people reflect Your character.

And if my life can help even one person step out of darkness and into Your light, then let me faithfully carry Your presence wherever You lead me.

I am Yours.

Let my life reflect You well.

Amen

Rabbit Trail 23 — Free Indeed

John 8:36

So if the Son sets you free, you are truly free.

There is something in that verse that reaches deeper every time I sit with it.

Not just free.

Truly free.

Actually free.

In reality free.

Not pretending.

Not almost.

Not temporarily.

Not free on good days and enslaved on bad ones.

Free indeed.

And that matters, because before Christ, I may have thought I was making my own choices, running my own life, steering my own ship—but the truth is, outside of Him, I was a slave to sin. Maybe not always in loud, obvious ways. Maybe sometimes in polished, respectable ways. But still a slave.

A slave to fear.

A slave to self-protection.

A slave to pride.

A slave to appetite.

A slave to control.

And the hardest part of slavery is that sometimes it feels so natural you mistake it for freedom.

Jesus was not talking about surface-level relief. He was talking about a complete change of status. A complete change of identity.

A slave cannot make himself a son. A slave cannot work hard enough to become an heir. A slave cannot declare himself free and make it true.

Only the Son can do that.

That is what makes this verse so weighty.

The freedom comes from Him.

Not from my effort.

Not from my sincerity.

Not from how bad I feel about my sin.

Not from my trying harder to be better.

From Him.

And yet there is something on my part that matters deeply.

Surrender.

That is the thing standing between where I stand in slavery and the sonship He offers.

Not because surrender earns it.

But because surrender is how I stop fighting the only One who can free me.

Control keeps me enslaved longer.

That is hard to admit, but it's true.

As long as I cling to control—my opinions, my pride, my right to decide for myself what is good and what is evil, my insistence on managing my own salvation—I remain stuck in the very thing I say I want deliverance from.

But when I humble myself, when I stop trying to rule my own little kingdom, when I cry out to the Father and say, "I cannot fix this. I cannot free myself. I need the blood of Christ applied to me," everything changes.

Then the Son does what only the Son can do.

And when the Father looks at me, He no longer sees me tainted by sin. He sees me covered in Christ. He sees me as I was meant to be. Not because I became flawless, but because Christ made me whole.

That is freedom.

Not "as if" I'm free.

Free.

And I think one reason this matters so much to me is because I've seen little glimpses of this in ordinary life.

I've worked for elderly people for long stretches of time—helping with yard work, homes, daily stewardship, all the little details of their world. Over time, trust builds. They begin to rely on you. They bless you. It benefits you. You gain access and responsibility because they know you'll take care of their little kingdom well.

But no matter how much trust exists, there is often still an uncertainty.

Because eventually, there comes a point where that person may no longer be making their own decisions. Their heirs begin stepping in. And then the question quietly hangs in the air: Will they let me remain? Will they want me here? Will they trust me too?

There is a built-in insecurity when you are a steward without heirship.
You may be welcomed for a time.
You may be trusted for a season.
You may even be deeply appreciated.
But there is still uncertainty.
To become an heir is a completely different thing.
An heir belongs.
An heir is not wondering whether they will be dismissed when the household shifts.
An heir is part of the family.
And that is what Jesus does.
He does not simply improve my conditions as a slave.
He brings me into sonship.
He removes the uncertainty.
He does not leave me standing at the edge of the household hoping I'm still welcome tomorrow.
He makes me family.
That is why this freedom is so much bigger than pardon.
This is not just "you are no longer punished."
This is "you belong."
It is slavery to freedom to sonship.
And once I understand that, my identity changes.
I stop seeing myself as someone on probation.
I stop seeing myself as someone barely making it into the house.
I stop seeing myself as someone who has to keep proving I deserve to stay.

I am in Christ.

Christ is in me.

And because of His blood, I am not just tolerated in the Father's
house—I am a son or daughter there.

That kind of freedom changes how I walk.

It changes how I pray.

It changes how I see my failures.

It changes how I see the future.

And it stirs gratitude I cannot even put into words.

Because to go from slavery to true freedom to family… that is
not a small salvation.

That is everything.

Reflective Question

Where in my life am I still clinging to control in ways that keep
me thinking like a slave instead of living like a son or daughter—
and what would it look like to fully surrender that place to Christ
and walk in the freedom He has already secured for me?

Father,

Thank You that true freedom is not something I have to fake until I feel it.

Thank You that if the Son sets me free, I am truly free.

I know there are still places in me that want control. Places that want to manage, protect, decide, and hold on. And I see now that those very places keep me thinking like a slave.

I don't want to live that way.

I humble myself before You and ask You again to apply the finished work of Christ to every part of me. Cover me so completely that when You look at me, all You see is what Jesus has done.

Teach me to stop clinging to what keeps me bound.

Teach me to surrender more quickly.

Teach me to live like I belong in Your house.

Show me the places where I am still walking with uncertainty when You have already made me an heir. Show me where I am still living like I have to earn what You have already given.

Wrap my heart around this truth until it becomes how I actually live:

I am in Christ.

Christ is in me.

And I am free indeed.

Amen

Rabbit Trail 24 — Secure in Love

Romans 8:38-39

For I am convinced [and continue to be convinced—beyond any doubt] that neither death, nor life, nor angels, nor principalities, nor things present and threatening, nor things to come, nor powers, nor height, nor depth, nor any other created thing, will be able to separate us from the [unlimited] love of God, which is in Christ Jesus our Lord.

There are some truths that feel so big, so overwhelming, that it's hard to know where to even begin.

This is one of those.

Paul says, "I am convinced... beyond any doubt."

Not hoping.

Not guessing.

Not trying to believe.

Convinced.

And what he is convinced of is this:

Nothing—absolutely nothing—can separate me from the love of God.

Not what I've done.

Not what I will do.

Not what I feel.

Not what I fear.

Not what I understand.

Not what I don't.

Nothing.

And when I try to wrap my mind around that, I find myself reaching for something in my life that even comes close to resembling that kind of love... and honestly, the closest picture I can find is my mom.
She sees me clearly.
She doesn't ignore my shortcomings. She doesn't pretend I always get it right. There are times she will call things what they are. There are times she'll point out where I've fallen short or where I've made something harder than it needed to be.
But even in that, it is never wrapped in shame.
Never condemnation.
Always grace.
Always love.
Always this deep, steady desire for my life to be beautiful and whole.
She doesn't magnify my failures.
She doesn't define me by my worst moments.
Even when she's disappointed, that disappointment is saturated in love.
And as beautiful as that is...
It still doesn't even begin to compare to the love of God.
Because God didn't just feel love for me.
He gave everything for me.
Christ gave His life for me.
And now I am told—clearly, firmly, without condition—that nothing can separate me from that love.

Not even me.

And yet, there is something important to understand here,
because this kind of love can be misunderstood.

Just because love is unbreakable... does not mean relationship is
unhindered.

I can't make my mom stop loving me.

That will never happen.

But could I damage my relationship with her?

Yes.

Could I behave in ways that make closeness difficult?

Yes.

Could I create distance in how we walk together?

Yes.

Her love would never change.

But my experience of that relationship could.

And it's the same with the Lord.

There is nothing I can do that makes Him love me less.

Nothing.

But I can choose ways of living that affect my experience of
walking with Him.

I can resist Him.

Ignore Him.

Push against Him.

Choose my way over His.

And when I do that, it doesn't mean He withdraws His love.
It means I step out of alignment with the life He desires for me.
And sometimes that means access to certain blessings is limited
—not because He is withholding love, but because He is
protecting me.
Because just like a good parent doesn't hand over everything to a
child who isn't ready, God does not pour out what would harm me
or be wasted in the condition I'm in.
That's not rejection.
That's love, too.
As parents, we understand this.
We would love to give our children everything.
We would love to entrust them with the best of what we have.
But if they're not ready... if it would harm them... if it would
lead them further away instead of deeper into life...
We wait.
Not because we love them less.
But because we love them wisely.
And God's love is perfect.
So His love for me never wavers.
But His desire is not just that I know I am loved.
His desire is that I walk so closely with Him that nothing has to
be withheld.

That nothing has to be delayed.

That my life is positioned to receive everything He longs to pour out.

And that is what stirs something in me.

Because when I begin to even slightly grasp how secure I am in His love... it doesn't make me careless.

It makes me grateful.

It makes me want to walk more closely, not less.

It makes me want to align my life with His heart—not to earn His love, but because I already have it.

I want to walk in a way that says,

"I may not understand the fullness of this love...

but I am grateful for all of it."

I am in Christ.

Christ is in me.

And nothing—nothing—can separate me from the love of God.

That truth doesn't loosen my walk.

It anchors it.

Reflective Question

If I am truly secure in God's love—completely and unconditionally—what would it look like for me to stop striving for that love and instead begin walking in deeper alignment with it?

Where might my life still reflect distance when His love has never moved?

Prayer
Father,
I don't think I fully understand how much You love me.
But I know it is more than I can measure.
Thank You that Your love for me is not fragile. Thank You that it
is not dependent on my performance, my consistency, or my
ability to get everything right.
Thank You that nothing can separate me from Your love.
And yet, Lord, I don't want to just know that truth—I want to
live in it.
Show me the places where I am creating distance in my walk
with You. Show me where I am resisting what You are inviting me
into.
Not so that I can earn anything… but so that I can walk fully in
what You have already given.
I want to live close to You.
I want to live in a way where nothing You desire to pour into my
life has to be held back.
Teach me to walk in gratitude.
Teach me to walk in trust.
Teach me to walk in the security of being completely loved.
I am Yours.
And I am so thankful.
Amen

Rabbit Trail 25 — Rooted, Not Shaken
Colossians 2:6–7 (KJV)
"As ye have therefore received Christ Jesus the Lord, so walk ye in him:
Rooted and built up in him, and stablished in the faith, as ye have been taught, abounding therein with thanksgiving."

There is something I've noticed about being around certain people. Sometimes, without being able to explain why, their presence feels nourishing. It steadies me. It draws me in. Other times, being near someone feels brash or hollow, and I find myself eager to leave—not because they've said anything overtly wrong, but because something in their presence feels unsettled.
Identity carries a weight. It has an atmosphere.
I think of coffee. No matter the roast—light, dark, bold, mild—the moment I smell it, I know exactly what it is. I don't need an explanation. I don't need a label. That aroma reaches me before any words do, and it stirs something in me. Desire. Comfort. Familiarity. Nourishment.
Popcorn is the same. No matter where I am, if that scent drifts past me, I recognize it instantly. I may not have been thinking about popcorn at all, but the aroma awakens a longing. Something good is happening nearby.
Scripture tells us that when we receive Christ, we are to walk in Him—rooted, built up, established. Not frantic. Not striving. Rooted. And from that rootedness comes an overflow. Thanksgiving. Life. Presence.

What strikes me is that rooted things don't try to be noticeable. They simply are. And because they are healthy and grounded, something spills outward from them. An aroma. An overflow. Whether someone is newly walking with Christ or has followed Him for decades, the Spirit dwelling within them is the same. The depth may vary, the understanding may grow over time, but the essence—the presence of God—is unmistakable. Just like coffee, just like popcorn, the source is recognizable even when the expression differs.

This is not about performance or polish. It's not about having the right words or the strongest opinions. It's about whether what overflows from my life carries the aroma of Christ—peace, compassion, steadiness, truth, love—or whether I am so shaken that my presence feels sharp, hurried, or closed.

When I am rooted in Him, I don't have to announce my faith. I don't have to prove anything. The overflow tells the story for me. People may not know what they are sensing at first, but they recognize that it is nourishing. And that recognition invites them closer—not to me, but to Him.

Rootedness produces aroma.

And aroma invites hunger.

Reflective Question

When I step back and ask God to help me see clearly, what might He be gently revealing about the aroma and overflow of my life right now—and how might deeper rootedness in Him shape what others experience when they are near me?

Prayer

Father,

I come to You quietly, without defense or striving. I ask You to help me see myself through Your eyes—not to accuse me, but to reveal truth with kindness. Show me where my roots are strong and where they need to go deeper. Purify what overflows from my life so that it reflects Your peace, Your compassion, and Your love. Let the aroma of my presence be shaped by Your Spirit, not my restlessness or fear. Draw me closer to You, and from that closeness, let my life gently invite others toward what is good and true.

Amen

Rabbit Trail 26 — Walking Humbly With God
Micah 6:8 (NIV)
He has shown you, O mortal, what is good.
And what does the Lord require of you?
To act justly and to love mercy
and to walk humbly with your God.
There's something steadying about this verse.
It doesn't leave me guessing.
It doesn't leave me striving to figure it all out on my own.
It says—He has shown you.
Not, figure it out.
Not, decide for yourself.
Not, do your best with what you think is right.
He has shown you what is good.
And that right there corrects something in me that tends to
wander—
that quiet tendency to decide for myself what is just... what is
kind... what humility looks like.
Because if I'm honest, when I decide those things on my own, they
shift.
They bend.
They get shaped by what I feel in the moment... what seems
easiest... what keeps peace... what avoids discomfort... what
makes sense within my limited understanding.
But God is not limited.

He is not working within time like I am.
He is not working within partial information like I am.
He is not swayed by emotion, pressure, or perspective.
So when He defines what is good—
it is whole.
Complete.
True.
To Act Justly
Justice, when it comes from me, is often reactionary.
It's based on what I can see... what I understand... what feels
fair right now.
But God's justice is not partial.
It's not rushed.
It's not reactive.
It is full.
There are times His justice doesn't make sense to me right away.
Times when I would have handled something differently.
Times when I would have sped it up... softened it... avoided it
altogether.
But that's exactly why I can't be the source of it.
If I want to walk in true justice, I have to draw from Him.
I have to be willing to say,
"Lord, what is actually just here?"
—not what feels just... not what looks just... but what is just.
And sometimes that requires patience.
Sometimes it requires restraint.
Sometimes it requires courage.
But it always requires Him.

To Love Mercy
This one gets misunderstood easily.
Because we tend to confuse kindness with niceness.
Niceness says,
"Let's keep everything comfortable."
"Let's not stir anything up."
"Let's make sure everyone feels okay in the moment."
But kindness—real, God-formed kindness—looks further than
the moment.
Kindness is rooted in truth.
Kindness is willing to hold both grace and clarity at the same
time.
Kindness may say something hard...
not to wound, but to heal.
Because pretending everything is okay when it's not—
that isn't mercy.
That's avoidance.
God's mercy doesn't ignore reality.
It steps into it with love.
It sees the end from the beginning and acts accordingly.
So to love mercy means I don't just tolerate it—I value it.
I desire to reflect it.
I ask Him to teach me what true kindness looks like in each
moment,
even when it doesn't look "nice."

To Walk Humbly With Your God
This is where it all comes together.
And this is where I think we often get it wrong.
Humility is not being small.
It's not pretending I don't matter.
It's not letting myself be walked over.
It's not putting myself in harm's way just to avoid being seen as
proud.
That's not humility.
That's confusion.
Humility is this:
Knowing exactly where I belong.
And I belong with Him.
Humility looks like crawling up into His lap and saying,
"I don't have this.
I don't understand this.
I can't figure this out on my own.
I need You."
It's not weakness.
It's alignment.
Because when I am rightly positioned with Him,
everything else begins to fall into place.
When I am humble before God,
I am no longer trying to prove myself to people.
I am no longer trying to control outcomes.
I am no longer pretending I have all the answers.
I am simply walking—with Him.
Step by step.

Moment by moment.
Drawing from His justice.
Reflecting His mercy.
Resting in His guidance.
And that kind of walk...
is steady.
It's not frantic.
It's not forced.
It's not performative.
It's relational.
I am in Christ.
Christ is in me.
And walking humbly with God is simply living that truth out—
one surrendered step at a time.

Reflective Question
Where in my life am I quietly deciding for myself what is right,
kind, or necessary... instead of pausing long enough to ask God
what is true?
What would it look like today to step out of my own
understanding and walk more closely with Him in that place?

Father,
Thank You for not leaving me to figure this out on my own.
Thank You that You have already shown me what is good.
I don't want to define justice by what I feel.
I don't want to call something kind just because it's easy.
And I don't want to confuse humility with shrinking myself or
pretending I don't need You.
I need You.
In every conversation...
in every decision...
in every reaction...
I need You.
Teach me what true justice looks like through Your eyes.
Teach me how to love mercy the way You do—full of truth and
grace.
And teach me how to walk humbly with You, not as a
performance, but as a relationship.
Let me be quick to come to You.
Quick to listen.
Quick to surrender.
I don't want to walk ahead of You.
I don't want to lag behind.
I want to walk with You.
Step by step.
Held, guided, and steady in You.
Amen

Rabbit Trail 27 — Living as Citizens of Heaven

Philippians 3:20 (Amplified)

But [we are different, because] our citizenship is in heaven.
And from there we eagerly await [the coming of] the Savior,
the Lord Jesus Christ;

There's something in this verse that shifts everything if I
really let it settle in.

It doesn't say I will be a citizen of heaven one day.

It says I am.

Right now.

As I sit here.

As I walk through an ordinary day.

As I move through conversations, decisions, frustrations, joys

—

I am already a citizen of heaven.

That changes the way I see everything.

Because this isn't about me surviving earth while I wait to be
rescued.

This isn't about enduring this life until I can finally get to the
real one.

This is about living from heaven while I am still here.

I may not see the fullness of that kingdom with my natural
eyes yet...

but I carry the Spirit of the King of that kingdom inside of
me.

So heaven is not distant.

It's not detached.

It's not waiting somewhere far off to become relevant.

It is present.

And it is active.

In me.

That means my life isn't shaped primarily by what's happening around me.

It's shaped by who reigns within me.

It influences the words I speak—

because I carry the voice of a different kingdom.

It shapes the thoughts I allow—

because I'm no longer bound to the patterns of this world.

It guides the decisions I make—

because I answer to a higher authority.

It even affects the way I love people—

because I'm not just reacting to them... I'm representing Him.

And if I'm honest, some days that surrender feels light and joyful.

It feels natural to lean into Him... to follow... to trust.

And some days?

It feels like a wrestling match with my own impatience... my own pride... my own desire to do things my way, in my timing, with my understanding.

But even in that tension...

there is something beautifully overwhelming about the awareness of Him.

Because no matter what kind of day it is—

He is still reigning.

And I am still His.

And then there's this part—
"...we eagerly await the Savior..."
That word eagerly isn't passive.
It's not casual.
It's not distracted.
It's active anticipation.
And when I think about that... I can't help but remember
something simple and powerful.
When my son was little, we lived in a house where the front
window looked out over the driveway.
And every evening, during that last hour before his dad came
home...
he would plant himself at that window.
Completely fixed.
Completely focused.
Watching.
Waiting.
Anticipating.
It didn't matter what else was going on.
It didn't matter what toys were around him.
It didn't matter what he had been doing earlier in the day.
Everything in that last hour was filtered through one question:
Will I miss it if Daddy comes home?

And the moment he saw that car—
before it even pulled into the driveway—
he would erupt.
Jumping.
Clapping.
Squealing—
"Daddy's home!!"
Nothing else mattered in that moment.
Not his play.
Not distractions.
Not comfort.
Just the joy of seeing the one he loved most.

That's what this kind of anticipation looks like.
Not distracted.
Not half-aware.
Not occasionally remembering.
But living in such a way that everything I choose... everything I
engage in... everything I give my attention to is filtered through
this:
Will this draw me closer to Him... or dull my awareness of Him?
Because I am not just waiting for His return...
I am living in light of it.
I am living as someone who already belongs to Him.
Already carries Him.
Already represents His kingdom.

And one day—
what I have believed...
what I have carried...
what I have longed for...
will be fully seen.
Fully known.
Fully complete.
And until that day...
I want my life to reflect the truth:
I am in Christ.
Christ is in me.
And I am living right now as a citizen of heaven.

Reflective Question
If I truly believed that I am already a citizen of heaven—right now—how would it change what I give my attention to, what I tolerate, and what I pursue in my everyday life?
What might I need to shift so that I'm living with awareness, not distraction, as I await Him?

Father,
Thank You that I don't have to wait to belong to You.
Thank You that I am already Yours... already part of Your
kingdom... already held within Your presence.
Sometimes I live like I've forgotten that.
Sometimes I get distracted.
Pulled into things that don't matter.
Caught up in moments that dull my awareness of You.
But that's not where I want to live.
I want to live aware of You.
I want to live like my life is anchored in heaven, even while my
feet are on the ground here.
Teach me to carry Your presence well.
Teach me to speak, think, and choose like someone who belongs
to You.
And Father... stir in me that kind of anticipation—
the kind that watches...
the kind that waits...
the kind that doesn't want to miss even a moment of You
moving.
Let my heart be like that child at the window—
eager, expectant, full of joy at the thought of Your nearness.
And until the day I see You fully...
help me live in a way that reflects You clearly.
I am Yours.
And I am so grateful.
Amen

Matthew 28:18-20

Then Jesus came to them and said, "All authority in heaven and on earth has been given to me. Therefore go and make disciples of all nations, baptizing them in the name of the Father and of the Son and of the Holy Spirit, and teaching them to obey everything I have commanded you. And surely I am with you always, to the very end of the age."

There's something in this passage that has always made me stop and think.

Jesus says, "All authority in heaven and on earth has been given to me."

All authority.

Not some.

Not shared.

Not partial.

All.

And then—almost immediately—He turns and says, "Therefore... go."

That feels almost backward at first.

If He has all authority... why send me?

If He has all power... why involve someone like me?

Why not just do it Himself?

But that question begins to answer itself when I remember who I am now.

When I accepted what Christ did—

when I received His sacrifice...

when I surrendered my life and made Him Lord—

I didn't just receive forgiveness.

I entered into Him.

Christ is in me.

I am in Christ.

And I am hidden with Christ in God.

So when He says, "All authority has been given to me..."

and then says, "Therefore go..."

He isn't sending me out alone.

He is sending Himself—

through me.

That's where it shifts from confusing... to both beautiful and honestly a little overwhelming.

Because this isn't a casual suggestion.

This is a commission.

To go.

To make disciples.

To baptize.

To teach.

To walk alongside others and help them come into alignment with Him.

That's not small.

That's not light.

That's not something I can accomplish in my own strength.
And I think that's exactly the point.
Because left to myself…
I'm like a glove.
I have these garden gloves—soft, flexible, shaped for purpose.
But if I lay them on top of a shovel…
nothing happens.
They look like they should be able to do something.
They're formed for work.
But they have no power.
No life.
No ability to move or act on their own.
They are completely dependent on something greater entering
into them.
But the moment I slide my hands into those gloves—
everything changes.
Now they move.
Now they work.
Now they dig, plant, pull, build.
Not because the gloves suddenly became powerful…
but because they are now filled with the one who has the power.

That's me.
On my own, I'm the glove.
I can't transform hearts.
I can't bring life.
I can't open eyes.
I can't make anyone understand truth.
But when He inhabits me—
when I surrender...
when I allow Him to move through me—
then what He can do... begins to flow through my life.
Not perfectly.
Not flawlessly.
But genuinely.

And then He says something that steadies everything:
"Surely I am with you always..."
Not occasionally.
Not when I feel strong.
Not when I get it right.
Always.
To the very end.
So this isn't a commission followed by abandonment.
This is a commission wrapped in presence.
He doesn't say, "Go do this for me."
He says, "Go... and I will be with you."

So yes—this calling is big.
Yes—it stretches me.
Yes—it can feel intimidating at times.
But it is also deeply reassuring.
Because the responsibility is not to produce the outcome.
The responsibility is to remain surrendered.
To stay available.
To let Him fill the glove.
To let Him do the work.

And when I live like that...
this commission stops feeling like pressure...
and starts becoming purpose.
I am not trying to accomplish something for God.
I am allowing God to accomplish something through me.
I am in Christ.
Christ is in me.
And the authority He carries is not distant—
it is present within me...
moving, speaking, loving, and drawing others to Him.

Reflective Question
Am I trying to carry out God's calling in my own strength—like a
glove lying on the shovel—or am I intentionally surrendering each
day so that He can move through me and do what only He can
do?

Father,

This is bigger than me.

And I know that.

You've called me into something that I could never accomplish on

my own,

and honestly, that can feel overwhelming.

But thank You for not asking me to do this alone.

Thank You that You didn't just send me—

You came with me.

You are in me.

And I am in You.

Help me to stop striving in my own strength.

Help me to stop trying to prove that I can do this.

I can't.

But You can.

So I surrender again.

Fill me.

Move through me.

Speak through me.

Love through me.

Let my life be available to You in the ordinary moments—

in conversations, in decisions, in the quiet places no one else sees.

Make me aware that I am not empty...

I am inhabited.

And because of that, nothing You've called me to is impossible.

I trust You to do the work.

And I am grateful that You've chosen to do it through me.

Amen

Rabbit Trail 29 — Living From Love

John 15:9 (NASB)

"Just as the Father has loved Me, I also have loved you; remain in My love."

There is something so steady and grounding in that word—remain.

Not visit.

Not drop in occasionally.

Not return only when I've wandered too far.

Remain.

And when Jesus says that, He isn't describing something passive.

He's not saying, "Just sit there and do nothing."

He's inviting me into something active... intentional... continuous.

To stay.

To dwell.

To keep choosing Him.

Because remaining in His love is not automatic.

It's relational.

It's a continual choosing to trust Him...

a continual choosing to draw near...

a continual choosing to stay connected, like a branch to the vine.

Earlier in that same chapter, He gives that picture so clearly—
a branch doesn't produce fruit by trying harder.
It produces fruit because it is connected.
Because it is receiving life.
Because it is drawing from the source.
And the moment it disconnects...
the fruit stops.
Not because the branch lost its identity...
but because it stopped drawing life from where life comes from.
That's what remaining is.
It's not striving to be fruitful.
It's staying connected to the One who is life.
It's choosing, over and over again,
to lean into Him instead of into fear...
to trust Him instead of trying to control everything myself...
to believe that His love is steady, even when my emotions are not.
Because when I am truly remaining in His love—
fear begins to lose its grip.
I'm not afraid of losing Him.
I'm not afraid of falling out of His favor.
I'm not afraid of being cast aside.
Because I'm not performing for His love...
I'm living from it.

And then He says something that just reveals His heart so
beautifully:
"...so that My joy may be in you, and that your joy may be full."
That's the reason behind it all.
Not pressure.
Not obligation.
Not control.
Joy.
Full joy.
There is such kindness in that.
Even when He gives instruction...
even when He calls me to something...
even when it requires surrender...
it is always rooted in His kindness.
He is not asking me to remain in His love so He can take
something from me.
He is asking me to remain so that I don't miss what He is trying
to give me.

And when I begin to see that—
when I begin to recognize His kindness in everything—
even in the hard things...
even in the stretching...
even in the moments that don't make sense yet—
something shifts in me.
I don't have to force myself to remain.

I want to.
Because I trust Him.
Because I know His heart.
Because I've seen His kindness too many times to doubt it now.
And from that place—
fruit comes.
Not forced.
Not manufactured.
Not performed.
Just... produced.
Naturally.
Because I am connected.
Because I am receiving.
Because I am remaining.

I am in Christ.
Christ is in me.
And when I live from His love instead of striving for it...
my life begins to reflect Him without effort.
Not perfectly.
But truly.
And that is where joy becomes full.

Reflective Question
Am I trying to produce fruit in my life by effort and striving...
or am I intentionally remaining in Christ, trusting that staying
connected to Him is what will naturally produce what my life
needs?
Where might I need to shift from striving... to simply staying?

Prayer
Father,
Thank You for loving me the way You do.
Thank You that I don't have to earn it... chase it... or prove
myself worthy of it.
You've already given it.
And You've invited me to remain in it.
Teach me what that really looks like.
Because sometimes I drift.
Sometimes I strive.
Sometimes I try to produce things in my own strength instead
of just staying connected to You.
But that's not where I want to live.

I want to remain.
I want to stay close.
I want to trust You deeply.
I want to draw from You continuously.
Help me choose You—again and again and again.
When fear tries to creep in... remind me of Your love.
When I feel distant... draw me back gently.
When I start striving... quiet me and bring me back to simply being with You.
And Father...
thank You for Your kindness.
Thank You that everything You ask of me is rooted in love...
and that Your desire is not to burden me, but to fill me with joy.
Let my life bear fruit—not because I forced it...
but because I stayed with You.
I love You.
Amen

Rabbit Trail 30 — Who Am I? I Am His

Colossians 1:13–14

For He has rescued us and has drawn us to Himself from the
dominion of darkness, and has transferred us to the kingdom of
His beloved Son, in whom we have redemption [because of His
sacrifice, resulting in] the forgiveness of our sins [and the
cancellation of sins' penalty].

There's something about the word rescued that feels personal.

Not theoretical.

Not distant.

Not abstract.

Rescued.

And when I think about that, I can't help but go back to
something from when I was a little girl.

We were at the beach one day, and the jellyfish were in.

I don't remember if they showed up suddenly...

or if they had been there all along and I just hadn't noticed.

But I remember the moment I realized they were everywhere.

All around me.

And in my little five- or six-year-old mind, that was it.

Panic.

Fear.

Nowhere to step without danger.

That water, just moments before, had been fun and safe and full

of joy...

and suddenly it felt like the dominion of something dark and

overwhelming.

They didn't stand on the shore and call out instructions.

They came into the water.

Right into the middle of what I was afraid of.

One took one arm.

One took the other.

And they lifted me up—

so that not a single inch of me touched what I feared.

They carried me completely out of it.

Past the water.

Past the danger.

Into safety.

It's a simple memory.

But it gives me a picture.

Because that's what Christ did for me.

Only infinitely more.

I wasn't just surrounded by something that could harm me.

I was living in the dominion of darkness.

Under the power of sin.

Under the influence of what separated me from God.

Blind to what was true.

Bound to what I couldn't fix.

And I didn't have a way out.

Not one.

So He came in.

Not from a distance.

Not with instructions shouted from safety.

He stepped directly into what should have destroyed me.

And He didn't just reach for me—
He paid for me.
With His blood.

And when I received that...
when I stopped running...
when I stopped resisting...
when I surrendered and said, "Yes—You can be Lord here..."
everything changed.
Not gradually.
Not partially.
Completely.
I was transferred.
From one kingdom to another.
From darkness... into His kingdom.
From slavery... into freedom.
From debt... into redemption.
From condemnation... into forgiveness.
The penalty I owed—
canceled.
Not minimized.
Not ignored.
Canceled.

That means something for my identity.
It means I don't belong to what I used to be.
I don't belong to the shame.
I don't belong to the fear.
I don't belong to the sin that once defined me.
I am His.
Fully.
Completely.
Irrevocably.

And that truth does something in me.
It stirs gratitude that I don't think I will ever be able to fully
express.
Not just with words—
but with my life.
Because how do you respond to that kind of rescue?
How do you respond to that kind of love?

You live it.
You carry it.
You share it.
You look at the people around you—the ones who feel
surrounded...
the ones who feel like they've gone too far...
the ones who believe they are outcasts... condemned... unworthy
—
and you tell them:
He came for me... and He came for you too.

You show them—
not just with what you say,
but with how you love...
how you respond...
how you carry His heart into their world—
that they are not beyond His reach.
That they are not too far gone.
That even knowing everything...
He still chose to make the sacrifice.
For them.

And I don't live this way to earn anything from Him.
I live this way because of what He has already done.
Because I am in Christ.
Christ is in me.
And together—
we are hidden in God.
Hidden.
Protected.
Empowered.
Deeply... desperately... loved.
So when I ask the question now—
Who am I?
The answer is no longer complicated.
It's no longer tangled in performance or failure or perception.

It is simple.
It is settled.
It is secure.
I am His.
And He is mine.

⁂

Reflective Question
After everything I have seen, learned, wrestled through, and come
to understand—
Am I truly living as someone who belongs to Him?
Or am I still allowing old fears, old labels, or old ways of thinking
to define who I am?
What would it look like—today, in this moment—to fully
embrace the truth:
I am His... and I get to live like it?

Prayer
Father...
You have been so kind to me.
Through every question...
every wandering thought...
every place where I misunderstood...
every place where I tried to define myself apart from You—
You have remained.

You have pursued.
You have revealed truth to me, piece by piece, trail by trail.
And now I see it more clearly than I ever have before—
I am Yours.
Not because I earned it.
Not because I got it right.
Not because I proved anything to You.
But because You chose me...
You rescued me...
You paid for me...
and You brought me into Yourself.
Thank You.
Thank You for restoring what was broken.
Thank You for correcting what was distorted.
Thank You for showing me who I am—through Your eyes.
And Father, I don't want this to just be something I understand.
I want it to be something I live.
Help me walk in this identity.
Help me remain in You.
Help me reflect You clearly.
When I forget—remind me.
When I drift—draw me back.
When I struggle—steady me.
And use my life...
not perfectly, but genuinely...
to show others how loved they are.

Let everything I am...
everything I say...
everything I do...
point back to You.
Because You are worth it.
And I am so, so grateful to be Yours.
Amen